General editor: Graham Handley MA Ph.D.

Brodie's Notes on F. Scott Fitzgerald's

The Great Gatsby
and
Tender is the Night

Graham Handley MA Ph.D.
Formerly Principal Lecturer in English, College of All Saints, Tottenham

D1514052

Pan Books London, Sydney and Auckland

For Harry Butterworth,
in warmest regard and friendship.

Pan Books Ltd would like to thank the Estate of F. Scott Fitzgerald and The Bodley Head for their kind permission to let us quote extracts from *The Great Gatsby* and *Tender is the Night*. Our thanks also to Penguin Books for the use of their editions.

The Great Gatsby first published 1978 by Pan Books Ltd
Published with *Tender is the Night* 1989 by Pan Books Ltd
This revised edition published 1990 by Pan Books Ltd,
Cavaye Place, London SW10 9PG
9 8 7 6 5 4 3 2 1
© Pan Books Ltd 1990
ISBN 0 330 50293 X
Photoset by Parker Typesetting Service, Leicester
Printed and bound in Great Britain by
Richard Clay Ltd, Bungay, Suffolk

Contents

Page references in these Notes are to the Penguin edition of *The Great Gatsby* and the Penguin Twentieth-Century Classics edition of *Tender is the Night*, but as references are given to particular chapters the Notes may be used with any edition of the books.

For details about the Cowley edition of *Tender is the Night* see page 55.

Preface

The intention throughout this study aid is to stimulate and guide, to encourage your involvement in the books, and to develop informed responses and a sure understanding of the main details.

Brodie's Notes provide a clear outline of the play or novel's plot, followed by act, scene, or chapter summaries and/or commentaries. These are designed to emphasize the most important literary and factual details. Poems, stories or non-fiction texts combine brief summary with critical commentary on individual aspects or common features of the genre being examined. Textual notes define what is difficult or obscure and emphasize literary qualities. Revision questions are set at appropriate points to test your ability to appreciate the prescribed book and to write accurately and relevantly about it.

In addition, each of these Notes includes a critical appreciation of the author's art. This covers such major elements as characterization, style, structure, setting and themes. Poems are examined technically – rhyme, rhythm, for instance. In fact, any important aspect of the prescribed work will be evaluated. The aim is to send you back to the text you are studying.

Each study aid concludes with a series of general questions which require a detailed knowledge of the book: some of these questions may invite comparison with other books, some will be suitable for coursework exercises, and some could be adapted to work you are doing on another book or books. Each study aid has been adapted to meet the needs of the current examination requirements. They provide a basic, individual and imaginative response to the work being studied, and it is hoped that they will stimulate you to acquire disciplined reading habits and critical fluency.

Graham Handley 1990

The author and his work

Scott Fitzgerald was born in 1896 in St Paul, Minnesota, and was educated at Catholic schools and then at Princeton where, though he wrote much and took a major part in the theatrical life of the college, he failed to reach the academic standards required. From a very early age he wrote: plays, poems, stories; and ultimately, in 1920, he published *This Side of Paradise*, a loose but fascinating and original novel, which dealt largely with his life at Princeton. On the strength of its success he married Zelda Sayre from Montgomery, Alabama, and their tempestuous life together — they moved east and lived continually beyond their means — has become one of the legends of the Jazz Age, of which Fitzgerald has been called the laureate. If he was (indeed, he was much more than that), then Zelda was its golden girl. Both passed through the valley of the shadow of alcoholism, Scott emerging late in his short life safely on the other side, while Zelda succumbed to insanity in 1930, her periods of lucidity being few and far between. There is no point here in chronicling the personal relationship of these two tortured people, driven by what Nick in *The Great Gatsby* calls the 'hot whips': that they were jealous of each other is undoubtedly true; that they were in their different ways possessive and unpredictable, equally certain. But two admirable books from the range of anecdotal and sometimes unpleasant detail will carry the reader through each area of the story: Arthur Mizener's detailed, sympathetic yet balanced biography of Scott, *The Far Side of Paradise*, and Nancy Milford's rather more subjective account of Zelda in her *Zelda Fitzgerald*. Zelda's autobiographical novel *Save Me the Waltz* is also worth looking at. That she provided Scott with much of the material for his work is unquestionable. When their child Scottie was born, there is no doubt that Scott was the conventionally anxious expectant father; but he was also sufficiently alert to note his wife's reactions to the experience and to reproduce them in part in Daisy's account of the birth of her daughter in *The Great Gatsby*. That ability is perhaps the measure of the writer; and here we should consider briefly Scott Fitzgerald's contribution to the twentieth-century novel, leaving aside his career as a script writer, and with some regret ignoring the many fine stories he wrote.

Fitzgerald admired Conrad and Joyce, and there is little doubt that both influenced him, particularly in terms of style. The strength of Conrad's morality is certainly present in his work, and though the 'interior monologue' is thought to be Joyce's particular gift to his successors, we should, perhaps, concentrate more on Joyce's artistic dedication, his spare, refining quality apparent in *A Portrait of the Artist as a Young Man* and *Dubliners*. Stephen Dedalus was always conscious of words, and often lived through them, and we sense in Fitzgerald a similar pride in exactitude of expression. This is not immediately apparent when we come to *This Side of Paradise*: the later terseness of expression is used only occasionally here; the episodic movement of the narrative making for poetic and self-indulgent fancy as well as epigrammatic and ironic observations. The same is largely true of *The Beautiful and Damned*, though there are passages of highly sophisticated and refined writing: but it is not until *Gatsby* that the stream runs pure. The mirror is held up to the society of the time, but the reflection is an extraordinary one, for Fitzgerald saw clearly through the surface of life and penetrated not only into the social underworld but also into the underworld of the individual consciousness. Here his romanticism, cynicism and morality merge, and the result is an artistic and humanitarian coherence. He was never again to achieve quite that purity; and there is no doubt that his private life – with its anguished mental and emotional troubles and constant financial strain – took heavy toll of him as a writer.

Tender is the Night, which he regarded as his masterpiece, was published in 1934. Fitzgerald died in 1940 from a heart attack, but *The Last Tycoon* (unfinished) was published in 1941: it has a rich satirical and social power and one character, Monroe Starr, of outstanding originality.

Set beside his contemporaries Fitzgerald seems to be of incomparably greater stature. If Hemingway is the bullfighter, then Fitzgerald is the dancer; but no simple analogy will do here. Fitzgerald's line of inheritance is more properly from Henry James and Edith Wharton, though his is not the leisured writing epitomized by each of them. But Fitzgerald has this in common with the other two: a keen awareness of polished associative usage, a fine eye for the social nuance and an ear for the social effect or social solecism. They are all moralists, not because they attempt to redress the social evils they deplore, but because they inlay their work with unmistakable commentary. We understand why the enigma of Gatsby so fascinated Nick and, at the back of Nick, Fitzgerald; for the doors of society, eastern society, would have been closed to the young writer from Minnesota had he neither money nor reputation. Gatsby made the first and was on the edge of losing the second: Fitzgerald lost the first but posterity, in the form of literary judgement, has guaranteed the second.

The Great Gatsby
Editor's note

There exists a mass of material on Scott and Zelda, but in a sense that mass leads one from the text and into the tangled under-growth of another kind of fiction, that of literary personality. The following is an appraisal of a major novel, and if errors of emphasis do occur they are individual ones – doubtless the student who disagrees will find evidence in the text to support his view. No effort is made to trace the originals (Wolfshiem, for example) – this is a needless distraction from literary apprecia-tion; nor are the geographical references referred to in the Textual Notes. Westchester, Southampton and Flushing, together with the wider context of Louisville, Santa Barbara and New Orleans, can be readily discovered on maps of Long Island and the environs of New York, and the United States generally. West Egg and East Egg are light names for Long Island loca-tions, and the most interesting identification is Fitzgerald's own Note, 'Ash-heaps, memory of 125th, Great Neck', a reference to his own unhappy four months in New York in 1919; the ash-heaps were later cleared to provide a site for the New York World's Fair. Some textual points of interest are listed by Arthur Mizener on pages 380—1 of *The Far Side of Paradise*; the only one of importance for the reader of these Notes appears on page 62 of the Penguin edition, where Gatsby is balancing on the 'dash-board' of his car which, as Mizener points out, is a slip for 'running-board'.

Plot and background

The plot of *The Great Gatsby* is straightforward, though the tricks of the narration mean that the sequence of time is shifted somewhat to allow of a retrospective return to the courtship of Daisy and Gatsby – once by Jordan, and once by Nick himself recording a conversation with Gatsby.

James Gatz, who has re-named himself Jay Gatsby, falls in love with a Louisville belle called Daisy Fay, just before he goes overseas. They plan to marry, but after the armistice Gatsby spends a short time at Oxford and his return home is delayed. Daisy marries the wealthy Tom Buchanan and, after a honeymoon and continental tour, settles in fashionable East Egg with her arrogant and insensitive husband, who indulges himself with other women.

Meanwhile, Gatsby makes a great deal of money illicitly, largely through the agency of Meyer Wolfshiem, and buys himself a gigantic mansion at West Egg, from where he can see the green light of Daisy's dock across the bay. He nurtures the dream that one day they will meet again, and goes some way to arranging it through Nick. For a brief period there is the prospect of the dream coming true, but Daisy cannot deny her early love for her husband. The dream crumbles, its fragments spread in the dust of the road where Myrtle is knocked down by the car: Tom's car, driven by Daisy. To shield Daisy, Gatsby lets it be thought that he was driving – and is killed by Myrtle's crazed husband, who has been directed to his house by the vengeful Tom Buchanan. Nick organizes the funeral, which is attended only by Gatsby's father and the man with owl-eyed glasses who had marvelled at Gatsby's book collection.

In his novels Fitzgerald wrote about the East, though in the stories there is the occasional Minnesota setting. The romantic dream, the dream of riches, was to fascinate Scott Fitzgerald for the whole of his life, and he was to return to it as a theme again and again. In a sense, he himself was the permanent theme. The action of *The Great Gatsby* is set in the summer of 1922, the era of prohibition and hence of wholesale bootlegging, of gangsters and big parties. It was the time of a boom in motion pictures, though the era of the talkies was still a few years away; it was an era of increased sexual emancipation, of reaction against wartime austerity and the stricter moral code that had prevailed earlier; and it was the era of get-rich-quick. The real tumbling down did not occur until the Wall Street crash of 1929 and the subsequent depression. It is this permissiveness – somewhat paralleled today, we may feel – which Fitzgerald chronicles in the imperishable prose of *The Great Gatsby*. One understands the current interest in the period and in the novel, for particular decades have their own rhythms and sensibilities that speak to or are echoed by succeeding ones. But one wonders if the swinging sixties, or the moral dystrophy of the seventies, or the extremes of success and starvation emblematic of the eighties, have been recorded with the fine sense of perspective or the moral and artistic integrity that characterize and distinguish *The Great Gatsby*.

Chapter commentaries and textual notes

Epigraph to the novel:
Then wear the gold hat, if that will move her ...

Tom D'Invilliers is a character in Fitzgerald's first novel, *This Side of Paradise*, at Princeton with Amory Blaine. He is a poet, undoubtedly based on one of Fitzgerald's friends. The verse here is a direct if ironic comment on the career of Gatsby, who acquires the gold hat (money) and 'bounces' from the bottom to the top of society.

Chapter 1 (pp.7–25)

Nick is the narrator of the story and leads the reader back in time to a summer evening when he drove over to East Egg to have dinner with his cousin Daisy, her husband Tom and their friend Jordan Baker. He soon becomes aware of the fact that all is only superficially well between Daisy and Tom, for – according to Jordan's surreptitious information – the latter has a woman in New York. Daisy confides her unhappiness to her cousin. Nick returns to his modest 'estate' in West Egg, and notices his neighbour Jay Gatsby standing alone on the lawn of his mansion, stretching 'his arms towards the dark water in a curious way'; he appears to be trembling.

Note the quick establishing of character as Tom and Daisy are individualized. We are prepared for Tom's later violence – 'a cruel body'. There is a cloying emphasis on 'richness'. The dialogue is unforced and natural, the descriptions vivid, evocative, economical. Note the clarity and directness of the narrative method, and the ending of the chapter on a high point of mystery.

hostile levity i.e. a deliberate, off-putting light-heartedness (so as to avoid the confidences of others).
founded on the hard rock or the wet marshes The first of the natural images with which the novel is filled: here meaning resting on either a firm or an insecure base – the base being an individual's upbringing or code of morality.

to be in uniform ... moral attention forever The imagery is from the
First World War (1914–18), which America entered in 1917.

If personality is an unbroken series of successful gestures A superb
way of indicating what the world judges by – material success, giving
parties etc. An ironic definition.

what foul dust floated in the wake A unifying image implying
corruption but, as we read on, perhaps associated in the reader's mind
with the ash-heaps.

Dukes of Buccleuch From the Estate of Buccleuch in Selkirkshire, the
line can be traced back to Sir Richard le Scott (1249–85).

Teutonic migration Heavy irony to describe the German attempts at
expansion, which led to the Great War. Nick mentions the 'counter-
raid' – a reference to the Allies' resistance and ultimate triumph.

the bond business i.e. selling interest-bearing certificates.

prep school The equivalent of the British public school.

a pathfinder, an original settler This establishes links with the past, the
American traditon of building from nothing a new civilization – but
the tone is ironic too.

Midas ... Morgan ... Maecenas The first was the semi-legendary king
of Phrygia who was granted the wish that everything he touched
would be changed to gold; the second is the famous American
financier John Pierpont Morgan, a generous patron of art and
learning (1837–1913); the third an Etruscan who was the enlightened
patron of a literary circle that included Horace and Virgil.

the 'well-rounded man' Note the ironic tone – the implication being
that the more you know or learn about in the literary sense, the more
limited you are – because you have taken yourself too seriously.

slender riotous island Long Island.

a courtesy bay ... domesticated body Again the fine economical
statement. A 'courtesy' bay is one that hardly exists; 'domesticated'
here obviously means one that is much used.

white palaces The simple description conveys at once the exotic quality
of the houses and their separateness – the snobbery of their location
and their owners.

ends i.e. positions in an American football team.

for reproach i.e. for envy, for criticism.

two old friends whom I scarcely knew at all This underlines the
nature of the society described in the ever-present ironic tone. None
of Gatsby's 'friends' sticks to him in the end.

Georgian Colonial mansion Built in the style of architecture of the
period (1720–1830).

the lawn started at the beach For an analysis of this passage see the
section on *Style and its effects*.

fragilely bound An exquisite sense of texture is conveyed by the use of
this term.

pale flags ... frosted wedding-cake ... wine-coloured Economical and
imaginative metaphorical description.

were buoyed up as though upon an anchored balloon The whole of this paragraph should be carefully studied for the consummate effect achieved – an effect of movement and sound and at the same time possessing an ethereal quality.

as if each speech is an arrangement of notes that will never be played again The effect is illusory and Gatsby himself is to expose it when he refers to its 'money' quality.

throwing her body backward at the shoulders like a young cadet It is perhaps this kind of comparison which has led some critics to see 'homosexual' qualities in Jordan. In fact, it is her *athleticism* that is stressed.

as though he were moving a checker to another square Again indicates the range of Fitzgerald's imagery – the comparison suits Nick, who is not exactly a games player. (The Americans call the game of draughts 'checkers'.)

Slenderly, languidly, their hands set lightly on their hips The pose is typical of the time – and it also set the pattern for film shots.

in the absence of all desire They had no wish to do anything – an ironic comment in itself.

the white race will be ... it's been proved This indicates Tom's racial prejudice and his ignorance.

'We've got to beat them down' One of Daisy's few endearing qualities is her ability to be satirical at her husband's expense.

'That's why I came over to-night' This is part of a 'kidding' exchange between Daisy and Nick which provides a light antidote to the pompous and ill-informed seriousness of Tom.

like children leaving a pleasant street at dusk A fine natural image, in telling contrast to the artificiality of the Buchanans and their home.

It's romantic, isn't it Tom? Since Tom has just come from his call from Myrtle, Daisy is being heavily sarcastic.

the broken fragments of the last five minutes ... this fifth guest's shrill metallic urgency Telling imagery, for the novel is about the 'breaking' of people.

I'm glad it's a girl ... a beautiful little fool Daisy's words feelingly echo her own foolishness in marrying and being let down.

a flutter of slender muscles We are never allowed to forget that Jordan is a golfer. A 'flutter' would be associated romantically with the heart.

lock you up accidentally Daisy is 'sending up' the kind of romantic situations that occur in magazine stories.

Our white girlhood Daisy is deliberately mocking Tom's 'anti-black' ideas. She throws in a reference to the 'Nordic' race.

in a flower-like way Daisy has compared Nick with a rose, and the flower imagery which surrounds her (see the section on *Style and its effects*) is part of the ironic conception – the ephemeral nature of love and life – and dreams.

I reached my estate Nick has his own delicious sense of irony at his own expense.

wings beating in the trees ... the frogs full of life Once again, nature outside, with its own life, contrasted with the 'life' of boredom or pettiness within.

the silver pepper of the stars At the time of writing this was an imaginative observation; is now something of a cliché.

he stretched out his arms toward the dark water The first indication that there is something strange about Gatsby. Later we realize that he is looking towards the 'green light' where Daisy lives.

Chapter 2 (pp.26–40)

This opens with the superb description of the valley of ashes, overlooked by the eyes of Dr T. J. Eckleburg, the whole symbolizing the desolate land of poverty as distinct from the rich and plush surroundings of the previous chapter. This contrast is maintained in the visit to the garage. Tom is revealed as unscrupulous and hypocritical, playing Wilson along on the small promise. The drinking emphasizes his decadence, and the restless disillusion of the period. Note how the dialogue flows – like the liquor – and register too Fitzgerald's marvellous ear for the nuances of speech. Myrtle's sensuality is vividly conjured, as are the differences between herself and Tom. His brutality is typical of the man. An ironic humour plays over the whole party.

a valley of ashes See the section on *Style and its effects*. It is a waste land, a 'solemn dumping ground' effective immediately by way of contrast with the Buchanans' – and later Gatsby's – house. It symbolizes death, the worn-out materials of society and the worn-out people too, like Wilson, as we shall see.

Doctor T. J. Eckleburg Symbol of the blindness, sterility and desolation of the time, but later seen by Wilson as God, and thus a part of his mental delusion.

wreck of a Ford which crouched in a dim corner The standard American car of the time, but the interesting aspect of this is the personification, the animal-killer associations. Such a car kills Myrtle.

as if the nerves of her body were continually smouldering A fine way of conveying the sensual, physically vital nature of Myrtle.

setting torpedoes Explosive cartridges.

John D. Rockefeller American financier and millionaire, who made his fortune in oil. The irony of the resemblance is an indication of the inequality of men.

one slice in a long cake of apartment-houses A typical Fitzgerald imaginative association – Nick has just come from a 'rich' house.

the gardens of Versailles i.e. the tapestry depicted scenes of French Court life, probably of the period of Louis XIV.

sticky bob i.e. cut in the short style of the time.

appendicitis She means 'appendix', a sufficient indication of her lack of education, and perhaps a pointer to the reason for Tom's snobbery when she mentions Daisy's name.

Kaiser Wilhelm's The German Emperor's, i.e. the Emperor who plunged Europe into war in 1914.

gyped out of it . . . private rooms Cheated . . . private gambling.

to beat the band Excessively, greatly.

the casual watcher in the darkening streets Superb perspective, showing the awareness of life outside, and of other lives being lived just like these. In some ways Nick is the 'casual watcher' in the novel.

a black silk bow for mother's grave that'll last all summer A singular indication of how Myrtle in her life with her husband has to be economical.

Making a short deft movement Note the sudden, fine economy of the sentence which fits the swiftness of the blow.

Beauty and the Beast Titles of pictures by McKee in his portfolio. Perhaps consciously Nick carries over the titles to the real-life experience of Pennsylvania Station in the morning.

Chapter 3 (pp.41–60)

This opens with a description of the preparations for a lavish Gatsby party. One night Nick is invited over to his neighbour's, re-meets Jordan Baker, describes the society present but only inadvertently gets to meet his host. Before that happens there is much talk of Gatsby and his supposed past. Nick observes the party and the characters attending it. Then he walks 'across the lawn toward home'.

The party atmosphere here contrasts effectively with the sleazy atmosphere of the previous section. It is extravagant, the restless need of society to be entertained and to escape from humdrum existence. It is graphic and poetic too, coloured by Nick's ironic observation. It is strongly visual, loudly compelling. But with regard to Gatsby himself there is an air of mystery – an unvoiced suggestion of shady dealing beneath the glitter. Nick is obviously caught up in the marvel of the spectacle (and his thoughts of Jordan Baker too). The post-war world harks back to the war. This is the escape of the rich from it. The unique and enigmatic quality of Gatsby comes over at once in his smile and in the contrasts his personality presents. The car incident anticipates the ever-present irresponsibility which kills Myrtle.

Nick records briefly the events of his own life, having observed that the affairs of Gatsby 'were merely casual events in a crowded summer'. He recalls his liking for New York, his thoughts of Jordan Baker, his learning that she was a liar; on occasions he drove out with her, but felt that he 'must get myself definitely out of that tangle back home'.

like a brisk yellow bug The simile implies a certain parasitic quality – not inappropriate, since Gatsby is surrounded by parasites.

The last swimmers have come in from the beach now Note the effective transition into the present tense which gives graphic immediacy to the scene.

the sea-change of faces and voices and colour i.e. the transformation wrought by the light etc. The derivation is from *The Tempest* I, 2, 400 (Ariel's song).

Gilda Gray's understudy from the Follies i.e. the stand-in for the star of a musical show.

swirls and eddies of people Linked with 'sea-change' above.

Croirier's Fashionable store.

its spectroscopic gaiety i.e. its ability to measure the quality of the gaiety, the party.

probably transported complete from some ruin overseas Heavy irony at the expense of the *nouveaux riches* who buy anything, however ugly, that smacks of tradition. Fitzgerald knows too well the 'culture' tendencies of some of his countrymen.

with enormous owl-eyed spectacles Notice the parallel with Dr T. J. Eckleburg; the latter motivates Wilson to destructive force, but this man is the only one, Nick and Mr Gatz apart, who comes to Gatsby's funeral.

Stoddard lectures Published 1897–98; the author was a travel lecturer.

Belasco (1853–1931). The American playwright, actor and theatrical manager.

didn't cut the pages The irony is the owl-eyed man's – you have to 'cut' the pages in order to read the book!

Mrs Claud Roosevelt At that time the name would be sufficiently famous (and wealthy) to get anyone into a party.

trembling a little to the stiff, tinny drip It is not merely the music that provides the effect of trembling, but the alcohol consumed as well.

something significant, elemental, and profound The comment is really a cynical one – Nick knows that when sober he will realize the emptiness of it all.

It was one of those rare smiles . . . an elegant young rough-neck This paragraph and Nick's reactions underline the duality of the Gatsby personality – the person he has tried to become in the quest for Daisy, and the person he has had to be in order to get the money to make the quest, the dream, possible.

on the wire Telegraph.

an urban distaste for the concrete i.e. the townsman's dislike of anything definite – gossip is preferable to what may be unwelcome facts.

At small parties there isn't any privacy At first sight, a contradiction; but perhaps there is truth in it – in a small group you are liable to be monopolized by someone you dislike.

echolalia Meaningless repetition, sound above sense.

Carnegie Hall Famous concert hall in New York.

Vladimir Tostoff's Jazz History Fitzgerald is parodying the somewhat pretentious compositions of the Jazz Age.

no French bob touched Gatsby's shoulder i.e. hair done in the latest Parisian style – but the important point here is the *isolation* of Gatsby from people (the dream is the be-all and end-all for him) *and* from what he has created.

like an angry diamond Sudden image, the 'flashing' reflection indicating the temper.

old sport Gatsby's phrase, imitated from the upper class English slang. It is his attempt to get himself 'right' socially.

explained the criminal The mere use of the last word underlines the moral condemnation involved.

A sudden emptiness seemed to flow The size of the house, and the isolation of Gatsby, give the aftermath of the party a deliberate pathos.

white chasms Nature referred to again by comparison – i.e. the streets between the huge buildings.

Sometimes, in my mind, I followed them to their apartments From being the narrator Nick has taken on a life of his own; this reveals the quality of his – and his creator's – imagination.

the Forties i.e. streets in that range of numbers.

a bad lie i.e an unfavourable position.

on a plane where any divergence from a code Jordan prefers easy-going, unintellectual men who are not going to probe motives or look too closely beneath the surface.

she passed so close to some workmen that our fender flicked a button This is a considered stress on the difference between the rich and the poor – and again there is the threat of a car accident. A fender is a bumper.

full of interior rules that act as brakes on my desires Nick means, and it is a touching assertion, that he has difficulty in committing himself. But note the image – brakes – which again links with the world of the car.

I am one of the few honest people that I have ever known There is no ring of complacency about this, and I think we accept the statement, at the same time noting that not doing something until you have cleared up something else is honesty on your own terms.

Chapter 4 (pp.60–78)

Nick gives a list (the author's satirical intention behind it is obvious) of the people who came to Gatsby's house that summer – their names have an almost Dickensian (though naturally Americanized) flavour. Gatsby tells Nick an elaborate story of his own antecedents, education, travels, and all of it has the unconvincing ring of falsehood. Gatsby seems to have undertaken this self-disclosure because of the confidence he wishes to impart to Nick about Daisy, and because he wishes to enlist his aid. Nick is initially cynical, then Gatsby begins to enlarge upon his wartime experiences.

At lunch Nick meets Gatsby's associate, Mr Wolfshiem, who reminisces about the past and makes particular reference to the killing of one Rosy Rosenthal. When Gatsby leaves to make a telephone call Wolfshiem tells Nick of his protégé's 'Oggsford' days, and Nick notices his cuff buttons made from human molars. Gatsby confides to Nick that Wolfshiem 'fixed the World's Series back in 1919'. Then, unexpectedly, they meet Tom Buchanan and after the introduction Gatsby leaves abruptly. Later Jordan tells Nick how, in 1917, Gatsby and Daisy fell in love.

This chapter is one of revelations – all the background material (with the exception of the exact nature of what Gatsby does, which remains a mystery) is important – and this use of retrospect is integral to the narrative. The contrast of sensitivity and toughness in Gatsby is again emphatic. Wolfshiem and Jordan have functional roles here. Shady dealing vies with the pathos of unhappiness for pride of place. The plot now hinges on Gatsby's need to meet Daisy.

bootlegger One dealing in illicit liquor, smuggling.
Von Hindenburg German Chief of Staff in the First World War, then President of the German Republic, 1925–34.
From East Egg, then, came the Chester Beckers For an analysis of this list see the section on *Style and its effects*. It is a sustained piece of mockery of American society, made all the more ridiculous by the choice and range of the names, which sometimes carry animal associations and sometimes pretentious literary ones. The interested student will examine, for example, names like Voltaire and Civet, the latter a carnivorous quadruped somewhere between a fox and a weasel in size – and it smells! There is a running wit throughout, but the general effect is of a description of decadence, of violence, drinking,

promiscuity, snobbery. Names that would repay investigation, to show the ironic effect Fitzgerald achieves, are Endive, Stonewall Jackson, Ulysses. Many of the other coinages and associations are witty because of their down-to-earth nature or their parody of pretentious associations.

Associated Traction would have to fluctuate profitably next day A satirical aside on corrupt practices in the stock market.

who killed himself by jumping in front of a subway train Note the incidence of death and accident in this account, symptomatic of a sick society.

their last names were either the melodious names of flowers Again, the flower *motif* running through *The Great Gatsby*, emphasizing the transitory, the ephemeral, as here, of society.

the American Legion An organization of veterans of World War I and World War II, founded in 1919.

caramel-coloured suit His clothes are always too elaborate – and detract from the effect of breeding he wishes to convey.

a turbaned 'character' leaking sawdust ... as he pursued a tiger through the Bois de Boulogne A reference to the 'rajah' and the false nature of Gatsby's account of himself. The Bois de Boulogne is a park on the outskirts of Paris.

Orderi di Danilo The order of Danilo.

Nicolas Rex i.e. King Nicolas.

Trinity Quad i.e. in the quadrangle of Trinity College Oxford.

the Earl of Doncaster This mention by Gatsby is another attempt to give himself status, this time through aristocratic connections.

faded-gilt nineteen-hundreds A reference to the style of decoration and ornamentation of the time.

the city rising up across the river in white heaps and sugar lumps all built with a wish out of non-olfactory money 'Olfactory' means 'concerned with smell', so the implication of this statement is that it is an ideal place – sugar lumps indicate sweetness – when seen from a distance that hides the corruption beneath.

A dead man passed us in a hearse Another superb anticipation, here by contrast, of Gatsby's own largely unmourned funeral.

driven by a white chauffeur ... three modish negroes A sign of the coming times, reminding us deliberately of Tom's racialism and his fears.

Katspaugh Note the name and the spelling. A 'catspaw' is a person used as a dupe or tool by another.

Oggsford College Wolfshiem is showing ignorance – Oxford has many colleges.

Finest specimens of human molars Perhaps a comment on the cannibalistic nature of society – the teeth worn as trophies seem, here, to be a reversion to primitive practice.

a denizen of Broadway Here it means a frequenter of the theatres and clubs, with perhaps an emphasis on the disreputable rather than the legitimate.

the World's series i.e. the leading baseball tournament.

fixed i.e. by bribery, corruption, a result is ensured that would pay off for a gambler like himself.

a strained unfamiliar look Explainable simply – he has just met Daisy's husband.

the red, white and blue banners . . . *tut-tut-tut-tut* The implication is that people might disapprove of her skirt blowing up.

and as drunk as a monkey A cliché expression. Jordan is not strong on original thought or language.

coming to pieces like snow Good simile in terms of what happens to the paper, but the texture is completely different.

Cannes . . . Deauville French tourist and pleasure resorts.

there's something in that voice of hers Jordan's remark anticipates Gatsby's precise definition later.

victoria Low, light, four-wheeled carriage.

I'm the Sheik of Araby Popular song of the time. Notice how the words echo Gatsby's dream – see the section on *Style and its effects*. There is something innocent about the children's song, just as there is about Gatsby's dream.

delivered suddenly from the womb of his purposeless splendour A fine image, and one is tempted to see it connecting with Daisy's little girl in a strangely ironic way. Birth should be wonderful, and the rearing of the dream is; by contrast, think back to Daisy's reaction to the birth of her child.

Her wan, scornful mouth The description sufficiently indicates Jordan's incapacity for 'love', and perhaps there is an ironic comment too on Nick's acceptance of this situation. It may reflect his own loneliness.

Chapter 5 (pp.79–93)

Nick invites Daisy to tea. When the day arrives it is pouring with rain. Nick leaves Daisy and Gatsby together, finds that they are hardly communicating with each other, goes outside and is followed by Gatsby; he urges the latter to return to Daisy, for he feels that Daisy is embarrassed. Nick remains outside, under a tree in the rain, staring at Gatsby's great house, but after half an hour he goes back in to find a changed situation – a glowing Gatsby, and Daisy's face 'smeared with tears', apparently of happiness. After this, all three go over to Gatsby's house. The ensuing tour is calculated to show off everything, from the 'Merton College library' to the display of shirts from 'a man in England who buys me clothes'. They go through the grounds, then back indoors to see Gatsby's 'clippings' of Daisy, and Klipspringer plays the piano for them at his host's insistence. The song with the line 'The rich get rich and the poor get – children' is particularly significant. Nick goes out into the rain yet again and leaves Gatsby and Daisy together.

The whole sequence is full of pathos, the weather acting as corollary to the tension felt by Gatsby (particularly) and Daisy. Nick's role here is functional, to bring the pair of them together. The initial artificiality is superbly conveyed, the change in the atmosphere on Nick's return is warm and moving. At the same time, one feels that Gatsby is lying. Nick is obviously sympathetically involved in the events. We sense already that although he knows that Gatsby is involved in criminal activities, he is moved by his suffering and the loyalty of his love.

the World's Fair Exhibition of the world's arts, crafts and inventions.

silver shirt and gold-coloured tie Although the suit is tasteful, one can argue that this is another sign of deliberate extravagance calculated to impress Daisy.

bleared windows Fine description, normally applied to eyes.

Castle Rackrent Nick, of course, is ready with the literary reference, here to Marie Edgeworth's novel of that name, about absentee landlords, published in 1800.

Does the gasoline affect his nose? Nick is implying that the chauffeur's nose is in the air, that he is being snobbish at having to deliver Daisy at such an unprepossessing house. It also connects with Daisy's story in Chapter 1 about the butler's nose.

as if he were on a wire Like a puppet.

a strained counterfeit i.e. a tense imitation.

a deep tropical burn i.e. a blush (of embarrassment).

well-shaved by Gatsby's gardener Note how things (here the lawn) are treated as people (shaved), the imagery reflecting the standards, misguided ones, of society.

like Kant at his church steeple Immanuel Kant (1724–1804), the German philosopher who looked at a church steeple to help his thoughts, and when the trees grew too large the tops were cut off so that he could continue to meditate profitably.

even eager, to be serfs ... been obstinate about being peasantry Again evidence of Fitzgerald's sure delicacy of touch. Serfs are attached to the soil, but here the implication is that Americans must have the security of the capitalist system, they must be slaves, while retaining the illusion of independence – i.e. not peasants.

full of aching, grieving beauty, told only of her unexpected joy The paradox of her reaction is perhaps expressed by the fact that she realizes that she *is* loved – and realizes too what she has lost.

feudal silhouette i.e. the outline, but the implication of a place employing many retainers, of subscribing to the old feudal system, contains an economical ironic thrust.

Restoration Salons i.e. in the style of the Restoration (1660) and after; drawing-rooms, reception rooms.

an Adam's study i.e. in the decorative style of the brothers Adam in the eighteenth century.

Chartreuse A liqueur made at the Carthusian monastery near Grenoble.

to see the rubies Nick is recurring ironically to the story of his life – the 'young rajah' account – which Gatsby had given him earlier.

made them feel more satisfactorily alone Apparently paradoxical, but not if one thinks about it – they are still too uncertain to be left alone.

In the morning The song sounds one of the themes of the novel – the contrast between the rich and the poor – and it looks back ironically to the 'poor boy' (Gatsby) and his love for the girl who needs to be 'rich'.

of a profound human change Sufficiently defined by Nick's commentary on men coming home for the evening.

when Daisy tumbled short of his dreams . . . the colossal vitality of his illusion . . . a creative passion . . . what a man can store up in his ghostly heart This paragraph, and the rest of the chapter, should be read closely. The sympathy of the narrator is with Gatsby from now on, regardless of the judgements of society. Fitzgerald creates the intensity of the atmosphere superbly, and the implication is that what is real to each of us – in Gatsby's case his dream – is much more real than the transitory life we have to live.

Chapter 6 (pp.94–107)

A reporter calls to find out from Gatsby whether anything is wrong, and Nick uses this as a lead-in to Gatsby's earlier life-style. Again the use of retrospect, here on Gatsby's past, is employed to achieve integration. Rich description attends James Gatz's dream, the driving ambition here ironically seen as the American way of life which is moral death. We note that Gatsby's story itself is a mark of his confiding respect for Nick.

Returning to the present, Tom and two friends drop in on Gatsby. The class difference between Tom and Gatsby is given a considered stress, and we note Tom's snobbery and his condescension. Whatever Gatsby has done – is doing – does not deflect our sympathies from him. There is considerable humour in the description of Gatsby's party and the reactions of the individual guests. Tom is of course intent on the exposure of Gatsby.

Afterwards, Nick waits up to talk to Gatsby, who points out

that Daisy didn't enjoy the party. He reveals that he wants Daisy to go to Tom and say that she never loved him, and he cherishes the romantic idea that afterwards they will go back to her house in Louisville and be married from there. Thus Gatsby recurs to the past, to the incredible beginning of the dream.

underground pipe-line to Canada Nick refers to this as a contemporary legend, perhaps equivalent to the Channel tunnel in our time.

sprang from his Platonic conception of himself From Plato the Greek philosopher who died in 347 BC. What it means here is that Gatsby lived up to the image he set for himself – and that image meant the acquisition of material wealth, 'a vast, vulgar and meretricious beauty'.

A universe of ineffable gaudiness . . . soaked with wet light his tangled clothes upon the floor He dreamed of riches and the trappings that go with them.

the unreality of reality . . . the rock of the world was founded securely on a fairy's wing A poetic way of saying that life – reality – is as nothing compared with dreams, the stuff of the future.

Madame de Maintenon (1635–1719). Mistress and then second wife of Louis XIV.

the vague contour . . . the substantiality of a man The vague outline in his mind had become real – he had grown up into what he dreamed of being.

That so? The conversation between the Sloanes, Gatsby, Nick and Tom is in fact a brilliant parody by Fitzgerald of non-communication, of people speaking on different levels, half hearing or not hearing at all, and using cliché responses.

Or present a green card Daisy 'kids' Nick constantly, but it is a reflex of her own 'sophistication'. She is mocking novelettes or, perhaps, conventions of behaviour.

his graceful, conservative fox-trot The dance-band standby of the time – Gatsby has at any rate acquired this social grace.

A fellow's getting off some funny stuff i.e. something amusing is happening – but really it is Tom's excuse to strike up a flirtation with a girl who Daisy describes as 'common but pretty'.

Miss Baedeker Satirically chosen name, since Baedekers produced the standard guides for European travel.

who rouged and powdered in an invisible glass i.e. because it cannot be seen through the dressing-room blind.

dilatory limousine i.e. late car.

just as if it were five years ago This insistence that the past can be wiped out is, of course, the beginning of the end of Gatsby's dream.

a desolate path of fruit rinds Compare this with the ash-heaps, for this too is a dumping-ground, in which the present soon becomes the past.

You can't repeat the past Of course Nick is right, and it is Gatsby's insistence that he *can* that brings about his fall.

**really formed a ladder and mounted to a secret place above the trees
. . . he could suck on the pap of life, gulp down the incomparable
milk of wonder** Again the childbirth image, this time to define the
'creative' aspect of Gatsby's dream. But there is an ironic association
too, for Gatsby is shortly to meet the child he cannot believe exists:
Daisy's little girl.

would never romp again like the mind of God That with his love for
Daisy his egoism would be in abeyance – that he would do things for
her in the future.

she blossomed for him like a flower The use of the ironic image yet
again, the stress on the ephemeral.

an elusive rhythm, a fragment of lost words This is a fascinating
moment in the novel; for we all at some moments in life tremble upon
the threshold of truth, on an insight that is there and yet not there.
This is Nick's experience here.

Chapter 7 (pp.108–39)

There is an ominous opening to the chapter with the lights
failing to go on at the mansion: even more ominous are the
tough servants who have replaced the old ones. Our feelings are
once more with Gatsby when Daisy's daughter is shown off. Note
the use of the heat – contrast with the rain when Gatsby and
Daisy were brought together by Nick. This is almost a symbol of
their coming separation. But meanwhile Tom suffers too,
feeling 'the hot whips of panic' as he senses that he is about to
lose wife and mistress. The chapter is full of tension, the con-
flicts and differences are epitomized when Daisy cannot meet
Gatsby's demands that she unsay and undo the past. Tom of
course is still following his intention of exposing Gatsby. The
crisis of the car crash and the killing of Myrtle leads to the plot
movement of identities and blame which ends with the murder
of Gatsby by the crazed Wilson. Tom and Daisy come together
for survival at the expense of Gatsby. Their lives, particularly
Tom's, lack the pathos and the innocence which Gatsby's possesses. The end of the chapter is almost unbearable in its pathetic delineation of Gatsby's forlorn hope and trampled dreams.

his career as Trimalchio One of the projected titles for the novel was
'Trimalchio in West Egg'. Trimalchio is the vulgar worldling in
Petronius's *The Satyricon*, a mock-heroic version of *The Odyssey*.

automobiles . . . sulkily Once again the personification of the cars,
perhaps ominous in view of the fact that the killing of Myrtle is not
that far away.

caravansary . . . like a card house A caravansary is an Eastern quadrangular inn with a great inner court where camel trains put up.

That anyone should care Superb creation of atmosphere, and it is the heat in fact which precipitates the tragedy, with Daisy wanting to go in to New York.

The master's body? roared the butler Nick is showing how the excessive heat can act on the imagination – but there is also a hint of the cinema, a 'movie' scene here.

a tiny gust of powder rose from her bosom The rich have their own 'dust', a telling contrast with the dust that rises from the ash-heaps.

to clog i.e. dance.

the well-disciplined child . . . four gin rickeys This time the contrast is deliberate: the child who is an ornament rather than a reality, goes out as the drinks – part of the 'sophistication' of life – come in. 'Rickeys' are made of carbonated water, lime juice and gin.

the earth's going to fall into the sun Tom immediately reveals that he doesn't know what he is talking about and the implication is that he is in some ways representative of his society.

What'll we do . . . and the day after that, and the next thirty years? The *ennui* of the idle rich is captured in these words, and the contrast with the ash-heaps that is built into the text is all the more apparent. The song played through the film version of *The Great Gatsby* began with the words, 'What'll I do, when you, are far away', an indication of the romantic emphasis that characterized the book's translation to the screen.

Her voice is full of money The sudden statement brings home the realization of the kind of music he has been listening to – not only to Gatsby but to Nick too.

High in a white palace the king's daughter The romance, the dream, the fairy story – and now the reality.

standard shift i.e. standard gears.

I can stop at a drug store Tom is getting at Gatsby – saying in fact that anything, even what is illicit, can be bought there.

circus wagon A reference to its ostentation, its showiness, the implication being that it is not a 'proper' car.

the edge of theoretical abyss i.e. he cannot develop any argument and so is near the 'abyss' of failure.

a medium i.e. a spiritualist, one who conducts seances.

there was no difference . . . so profound as the difference between the sick and the well Wisdom is scattered throughout *The Great Gatsby*, but this is one of the truths which is borne out in the action – Wilson's mental sickness takes a tragic turn for the worse.

kept their vigil Ironic, in view of the fact that later to Wilson they seem to be watching over him and conveying to him a message.

something very sensuous about it Unusual language for Jordan – but she is beginning to be drawn towards Nick, at least on this languid day.

like a damp snake around my legs Again the image is appropriate, not merely to the heat, but to the 'snake' of the situation which is wound around them all as the confrontation tightens.

we'd better telephone for an axe Meant as a joke, but in the light of the tension, an ominous image.

crabbing Grumbling.

bumming i.e. cadging, getting home free.

his thick fingers together like a clergyman Appropriate image, in view of the fact that Tom is now 'safeguarding' morals.

and only the dead dream fought on The reality has killed it – the reality of Daisy's love for Tom is the past, for Gatsby has insisted – and believed – that it always belonged to him.

like ghosts, even from our pity A poignant, final way of indicating the end of the romance.

Before me stretched the portentous, menacing road of a new decade The sudden sensitivity when age – a particular time of life – comes to us all, but it is heightened here by the 'menacing road' that leads to sudden death.

the reassuring pressure of her hand Jordan, it must be said, has borrowed a little romance from Gatsby and Daisy, and gives every sign here of 'fancying' Nick, and with increased passion later.

The young Greek, Michaelis Once again this signals the use of the flashback technique, here with more subtlety, since it is a flash forward technique too, to Myrtle's death.

He was his wife's man and not his own Poignant and ironic though this is, we remark the equally poignant comparison: in a sense Gatsby is Daisy's man and not his own.

The death car For sheer graphic immediacy, these two paragraphs are among the best in the novel. Myrtle's death is reported with economy and with realism, the ironic tone stripped down to the facts, which speak so volubly of the giving up of that 'tremendous vitality'.

We saw the three or four The switch back to the present, but with a very effective sense of perspective – almost like the technique in the cinema of cutting from one scene to another.

A pale well-dressed negro stepped near But the ironic tone is back with a vengeance – it is a negro who corroborates Tom's identification of the yellow car, a master-stroke of chance in view of Tom's racial views.

Picking up Wilson like a doll Commonplace image, once again stressing the contrast between the two men. But the 'doll' kills.

He didn't even stop his car The sublimely ironic moment of the novel – Gatsby the bootlegger has, unknown to Tom, been true to his dream even in reality, for he has with true chivalry protected Tom's wife, who was the driver of the death car.

the luminosity of his pink suit Gatsby's lack of breeding and taste is apparent in his last contact with Daisy.

the sacredness of the vigil To Gatsby the dream is not ended, and he cherishes Daisy's wishes, or her imagined wishes.

watching over nothing The chapter ends on this pathetic note, for
Gatsby is outside the experience of Tom and Daisy within the house.

Chapter 8 (pp.140–54)

This chapter is characterized by poignancy. We know already
much of what Gatsby says, but it does not lessen the graphic
immediacy of his experience. There is a cruel irony in the fact of
his receiving Daisy's letter about her forthcoming marriage to
Tom while he is in Oxford so far away. The now common
flashback technique, the manner of Nick's narration, conveys
the inevitability – the cunning and the craziness – of what happens. We feel the hand of fate – but we also feel the inherent
nobility of Gatsby.

Then there is another flashback sequence to the early hours of
the morning (remember Gatsby's early hours) with Michaelis
trying to comfort the nearly demented George Wilson. Eventually Wilson's running hysteria tells him that Myrtle could not
fool God, but he is looking at the giant eyes of Dr T. J. Eckleburg
when he says this, perhaps sufficient indication that events have
caused him to lose his reason. At about ten o'clock in the morning Wilson leaves. He reaches West Egg about two-thirty, and
asks the way to Gatsby's house. Now we have a further narrative
switch to Gatsby's actions on the fatal afternoon. He goes to the
pool about two o'clock, asking the butler to tell him when the
expected telephone call comes through. It doesn't come, but
obliquely we are told that Wilson arrives to shoot him, and then
kills himself.

the invisible cloak of his uniform i.e. he might be revealed as poor
and penniless once the war was over and he was no longer an officer.
an impersonal government to be blown anywhere An accurate
statement of the unpredictability of war.
to the following of a grail i.e. following, questing for what is sacred.
The Arthurian tone is not accidental – Gatsby is a knight in terms of
chivalry, devotion and worship from afar.
bought luxury of star-shine The glamour of riches and, as the rest of
the paragraph underlines, all that 'wealth imprisons and preserves'.
gleaming like silver ... above the hot struggles of the poor At once an
echo of his own life and of the song he was later to have Klipspringer
play for them.
'Beale Street Blues' The fact that a 'blues' number is mentioned
heightens the poignancy here.

a yellow trolley A street-car.

I'm going to drain the pool today Ironic, since Gatsby would not have been in the pool to be killed by Wilson if the gardener had done as he wished.

You're worth the whole damn bunch put together In one particular sense Nick is right – the dream involved a kind of integrity.

ecstatic cahoots i.e. a happy conspiracy.

list of quotations i.e. the prices then current.

The hard brown beetles kept thudding Note this image, an unpleasant manifestation of the heat in a confined space.

She ran out to speak to him and he wouldn't stop Wilson is right – this is a moment of rare pathos, for deception is evil, and out of it comes evil.

That's an advertisement But Wilson believes that T. J. Eckleburg is God – by association this is an anticipation of the god of advertising that rules so many people's lives today.

He must have looked up at an unfamiliar sky Not only is this a superb piece of writing, frightening in its realism as it captures the effect of nature when the day has changed for us because of our personal suffering, it is also a structurally effective climax to the novel. For Gatsby, who has lost his dream, is killed by Wilson, who has lost his, and his reason too. He is indeed a poor ghost, 'breathing dreams like air' – they both are, and they both cease to breathe. So consummate is Fitzgerald's artistry here that, if we read it quickly, we miss the full force of the word 'ashen', which is at once descriptive of Wilson and of death, and recalls the 'ash-heaps', the dust to which man returns.

the leg of transit The path followed.

Chapter 9 (pp.155–72)

Nick is telling the whole story, we learn from the vantage point of two years after the events. He recurs to that day and its terrible details, with Catherine's assertion that her sister was happily married to Wilson and the general tone of the newspaper reports. Nick phones Daisy – she has gone away – then phones Wolfshiem, from whom he receives a non-letter that next morning. Then, after a phone call from a man called Slagle, he learns from Henry C. Gatz in Minnesota that he is coming up for his son's funeral. When he arrives he talks to Nick of his great pride in his son Jimmy; meanwhile Klipspringer calls and implies that he will not be able to get away for the funeral. Nick soon realizes that no one wants to know of Gatsby now that he is dead, and that all the party-goers and people like Klipspringer lived 'on the courage of Gatsby's liquor'. Next day

Nick goes to see Wolfshiem, who will not be involved in the funeral but tells Nick how he 'made' Gatsby. Mr Gatz, a pathetic and lonely figure, shows Nick the details of Jimmy's 'schedule' as a young man. But the man with the owl-eyed spectacles does come to the funeral, and makes the classic comment about the dead man: 'The poor son-of-a-bitch.' In the final section Nick mentally recurs to his, Gatsby's and Daisy's Middle-West heritage: he decides to go back home; takes leave of Jordan Baker (now engaged to someone else); and casually meets Tom Buchanan.

The pathos is insistent, particularly when we encounter Gatsby's father. The legitimate rich survive; the terrible conspiracy of fate through detail and manipulation is seen. The overall comment embraces the American way of life, with its inequalities which make for tragedy. The unlikely – the presence of the owl-eyed man at the funeral – is set beside the intransigent survival qualities of Tom. Nick's compassion is insistent throughout.

Lutheran Protestant sect. Remember that James Gatz had briefly attended a Lutheran College.

One of my most vivid memories Another switch, this time back to Nick's own life and his nostalgia for certain things: a settled childhood, the small towns of the Middle West which he knew and to which he will/has returned. As he ponders he realizes that the principal people he has written about 'were all Westerners . . . perhaps we possessed some deficiency in common which made us subtly unadaptable to Eastern life'.

on which lies a drunken woman in a white evening dress For one vivid moment we remember Daisy and her state before her marriage – and then we move on into the terrible anonymity of Eastern US life which is being stressed here – 'But no one knows the woman's name, and no one cares.'

He threw dust into your eyes An ironic image, again linking with the dust of the ash-heaps.

to buy a pearl necklace – or perhaps only a pair of cuff buttons A subtly ironic reminder of the cuff buttons shown by Wolfshiem to Nick – the teeth of the dead man – with Tom oblivious of the 'dead man' who is his responsibility: Gatsby. Remember, too, that much earlier Tom had given Daisy a pearl necklace.

incoherent failure of a house once more Houses cannot speak, and the transferred emphasis takes in its history, and the 'failure' of Gatsby, and of society.

the old island here that flowered Cleverly, Nick links the historical discovery, the dream of those who discover new lands – in this case a new world and a new civilization to be made, a dream realized – with Gatsby's dream, the world symbolized for him by the green light 'at the end of Daisy's dock'.

stretch out our arms further Just as Gatsby did, towards the light.

So we beat on, boats against the current It is a fitting image, bearing in mind the location of the novel, and it links indelibly the past and the present and the dreams that are in all of us.

Scott Fitzgerald's Art in *The Great Gatsby*
The characters

Jay Gatsby

It was one of those rare smiles with a quality of eternal reassurance in it, that you may come across four or five times in life ... an elegant young rough-neck, a year or two over thirty, whose elaborate formality of speech just missed being absurd.

The eponymous hero of the novel is initially an enigmatic figure, and remains so at least for many of the partygoers who attend, drink, stagger away and slander him. Born James Gatz, the son of poor farming parents in the Midwest, he drifts from job to job until he meets the millionaire Dan Cody, who is rough, tough, sensual and degraded, and who employs him to look after him both on board ship and through his brothel-cum-saloon life on shore. Unfortunately, Cody is the prey of self-seeking women and, having been left twenty-five thousand dollars, Gatz finds himself receiving none of it.

His name is already Jay Gatsby, but his own dream for himself is modified somewhat when, as an officer waiting to go overseas during the war, he meets Daisy Fay (he is stationed near Louisville) and falls in love with her, while realizing that she lives in a rather different social world. Daisy returns his love; but when Gatsby stays in Europe for some time after the armistice, she resumes her social habits – she has plenty of 'beaux' – and finally she marries Tom Buchanan. This is a bare summary of the Gatsby–Daisy affair before the dream takes over; and our own dealings with Gatsby, as readers, are dominated by the dream and its effects.

Perhaps we must continue the story, obliquely told in the novel, of Gatsby's being sponsored by Wolfshiem in illicit drug and liquor dealing, which enables him to build a fortune and to buy the mansion at West Egg that gives him the view of Daisy's green light at the end of her dock. The dream has taken substantial shape, and when Nick first sees Gatsby he is stretching out 'his arms toward the dark water in a curious way ... I could have sworn he was trembling'. This is enigmatic enough, and the conversations, or rather snatches of them, that Nick hears ('he was a German spy ... I'll bet he killed a man') deepen the mystery, which is a little clearer when Nick finds himself talking inadvertently to his host during a party. They had been near one another in the same division in France, and Nick is quick to register the paradox in the quotation that heads this character-sketch – that Gatsby has a strong and warming individual quality, but at the same time is trying to cover up his background or actions, both of which may be dubious.

Gatsby tries a kind of familiarity ('old sport'), but this fails to register with Nick. Because of Nick's connection with Daisy, Gatsby enters into an elaborate explanation of his 'young rajah' past, which does not fool Nick but which does have a certain pathetic quality. Yet he takes Nick to meet Wolfshiem, admits that the latter fixed the World's Series of 1919, and thus puts himself in a vulnerable position. This implies a kind of integrity or sensitivity, as if he trusts Nick despite, or even because of, the fact that he knows that Nick will see through him. Admittedly there is the half-bribe that he would like to do something for Nick, but we have no doubt of our own sympathetic involvement with him when he meets Daisy. His nervousness takes the form of seeing that everything is just right by the standards he thinks will impress Daisy. His sensitivity is shown on two counts: firstly, his assuring Nick that he wouldn't have to do business with Wolfshiem if he accepted his (Gatsby's) favour; and secondly, almost frighteningly, his near-loss of nerve just before Daisy arrives – 'I can't wait all day.'

The scene that follows is harrowing, showing Gatsby's infinite capacity for suffering, but this is relieved after his return to the room when Nick has been very firm with him. From then on he translates the dream into fact, showing Daisy all the things he has acquired for her with at times a naïve, almost splendid casualness: 'I've got a man in England who buys me clothes.' Nick too is sensitive, and he notices that the 'expression of bewilderment had come back into Gatsby's face, as though a faint doubt had occurred to him'. But he has 'thrown himself into it (the dream) with creative passion', and it has, in fact, become more than Daisy herself. Gatsby is true to the dream – he has this fine capacity for imaginative wonder – but the reality cannot measure up to it. With the coming of real adversity he reveals qualities not before apparent: obstinacy; self-will; an impractical (and selfish) insistence about the obliteration of the past; and an almost total inability to live in the present. He is romantic, and has always been determined to build something for himself. He is, to borrow the original title of *This Side of Paradise*, the romantic egotist, but he shows an inability to compromise that ensures the shattering of his dream.

Gatsby symbolizes the self-made man. But whereas self-made men are, for a number of reasons, driven by an overwhelming ambition to make money, Gatsby is motivated by only one reason – the need to win Daisy back. It is an incredible obsession, but none the less a moving one. It speaks of integrity, loyalty, devotion, qualities that the moralist in Nick values; but in addition to this Gatsby is the eternal outsider, the man who never makes it into the inner courts of acceptable society though he could buy up that society and forget it. Gatsby is sensitive enough to be aware of all this, and to try to acquire the trappings: the Oxford background, the furniture, the gloss of conversation. But his inherent vulgarity – the pink suit, 'the Merton College Library', the uncut books – all these register with the discerning as well as with the parasites, and Gatsby is condescended to but never accepted. Yet to the end he remains the knight serving his lady: he is reduced in the Plaza suite to having Daisy admit her past love for Tom; to defending himself prettily against accusations; to hearing his dream described as a 'presumptuous flirtation'; and to being pushed, with contemptuous complacent arrogance, into driving back with Daisy. Yet he takes the blame for Daisy's running down of Myrtle, and the secret – Nick apart – goes with him to his unmourned grave. His lonely vigil, waiting in the garden for Daisy's never-to-be-given signal, is one of the saddest moments in the novel. Nick is right; he is better than the rest of them. For despite all the corruption there is a quality of innocence about Gatsby, the quality that believes, and lives in the belief. He is deliberately seen in contrast to Tom Buchanan, who has had all the advantages denied to Gatsby. The boy from the small town in the Midwest makes it to the big-time and falls as quickly, and as unnoticed, as the stars who shot to drunken prominence at his parties: in this way, through Gatsby, Scott Fitzgerald is exposing the nature of the American dream, and the facile acquisition of wealth that leads to the wasteland of money without humanity. However, we feel for and with Gatsby, for his own human dream has qualities transcending the petty achievements of men.

Tom Buchanan

Now he was a sturdy straw-haired man of thirty, with a rather hard mouth and a supercilious manner. Two shining arrogant eyes had established dominance over his face and gave him the appearance of always leaning aggressively forward. Not even the effeminate swank of his riding clothes could hide the enormous power of that body . . . It was a body capable of enormous leverage – a cruel body.

Thus Tom Buchanan, surely the most unlikeable character in *The Great Gatsby*: the legendary football player now graduated to polo; wealthy, a snob, womanizer, drinker. Also a man of violence, the swing of his moods superbly captured by Nick in one brief sentence: 'The transition from libertine to prig was so complete.' Our introduction to Buchanan is not auspicious: we are told that there was 'a touch of paternal contempt' in his voice, and we come to feel that the word 'paternal' has been given an unconsidered stress. He is restless, conducting Nick on a very quick visual inspection of his 'nice place', but we soon learn the reason for his being on edge – he is expecting a phone call from his mistress. He is superior, never having heard of Nick's employer, but we later discover that he often doesn't listen to what is being said anyway.

He has an indolent, reflex capacity for causing pain – witness Daisy's black and blue knuckle – which can be translated into positive physical violence, as we see from the sudden and explosive force with which he breaks Myrtle's nose. He is a frightening example of what today would be called a 'racialist'; as he puts it, without reserve, 'It's up to us, who are the dominant race, to watch out or these other races will have control of things.' As Nick observes, it is as if his complacency 'was not enough to him any more'. The telephone call over, and the emotional temperature having, so to speak, increased, he remains somewhat sulky.

But when Nick accompanies him to meet his 'girl' we learn much more of Tom's nature. He patronizes Wilson, whom he despises, and buys Myrtle a dog with an arrogant decisiveness; at the ensuing 'party' (what a contrast with Gatsby's!) Nick learns that Tom has told Myrtle he cannot be divorced because Daisy is a Catholic. Nick is 'a little shocked by the elaborateness of the lie'. This reveals Tom's unscrupulousness and hypocrisy, his determination to live both his lives on his own terms: his inherent snobbery – his them-and-us attitude – is displayed when he breaks Myrtle's nose.

After these two early scenes we do not see Tom again for some time. There is the brief meeting with Nick and Gatsby, the Wolfshiem lunch encounter, and then the visit with the Sloanes to Gatsby's, where the latter's ill-breeding is all too evident to Tom. He gives his opinion of Gatsby without being asked, a singular example at this stage of the pot calling the kettle black:

'By God, I may be old-fashioned in my ideas, but women run around too much these days to suit me. They meet all kinds of crazy fish.' (p. 110).

Women, of course, have their place in Tom's world, but one strictly circumscribed by his own ideas and desires. He goes to Gatsby's party with Daisy, his arrogance and complacency well to the fore, covets a girl he sees with another party of people, but later asserts that Gatsby must be a 'bootlegger' to have got 'this menagerie together'. He adds significantly that he is going to make a point of finding out what Gatsby does. The crisis comes at the luncheon party, when he makes his usual non-conversation and then sees a look of love between Gatsby and Daisy. He cracks a little, makes an unpleasant remark about being able to buy anything at a drugstore, and lets Nick and Jordan know exactly what he feels during the drive to town. After the brief visit to Wilson's garage he feels, according to Nick, the 'hot whips of panic. His wife and his mistress, until an hour ago secure and inviolate, were slipping precipitately from his control.' (p. 131)

The row between Tom and Gatsby sees Tom emerging on top, for Gatsby's unwise attempts to make Daisy admit that she has never loved Tom are baulked by memories of her past with Tom. There is a late flowering of Tom's complacency, and he refers to Gatsby's 'presumptuous little flirtation'. Arrived at the garage he discovers what has happened, makes sure his yellow car is identified so that Gatsby will be blamed for the death; then weeps over Myrtle, calling Gatsby 'a God-damned coward'. Nick sees him sitting intently, his hand covering Daisy's, then meets him much later and – as he suspected – learns that Tom directed Wilson to Gatsby on the fateful afternoon. Tom, like Daisy, will survive it all – he has money, status, arrogance, insensitivity: all the qualities acceptable in a society which knows no one for what he is, judging only by what appears on the surface.

Nick Carraway

Even when the East excited me most, even when I was most keenly aware of its superiority to the bored, sprawling, swollen towns beyond the Ohio, with their interminable inquisitions which spared only the children and the very old – even then it had always for me a quality of distortion.

Nick becomes a positive character in the novel and, by his own judgement and reportage, certainly sets the moral tone. Since his narration runs throughout the 170 pages, one can only deduce aspects of his character as distinct from his function in the novel, which is to tell the story of Gatsby. He is not only a pathfinder, a settler; he is the typical young man coming East to do a job. Nick is cultured and, by buying the right books, makes some effort to do his job well. He is aware of the gap between culture and money, has a keen sense of relationships and the niceties of behaviour and conversation, and finds himself caught up in what he has not got – money. Being a neighbour of Gatsby's, and a cousin of Daisy's, he is both in the dream and outside it, but his sensitivity and penetration make him a participant rather than a spectator. This does not mean that he intrudes: rather the reverse, for he goes out and shelters beneath the black tree and surveys Gatsby's house while Gatsby and Daisy renew their love. Later in the afternoon he leaves discreetly when they are sitting with one another. He is early drawn towards Gatsby; makes a *faux pas* at the first party he goes to by not knowing his host; listens to Gatsby's elaborate lies about his past activities; is suspicious of Wolfshiem; and vows to free himself from his own entanglement back home. He is attracted to Jordan Baker, but becomes so interested and morally involved in the Gatsby affair that he neglects the opportunity to make love to her, and at the end of it all vows to return home – and does.

So much for Nick's role: as we know, he poses a number of questions. Like Gatsby, he is an outsider, placed there by his culture – one ventures to say that no one else in the novel would speak of El Greco (except, perhaps, McKee), and the Midas–Maecenas reference would be beyond most. Why does Nick reject Jordan? Is it merely because he sees through her, or is it because he is frightened of commitment? One could go on indefinitely speculating about Nick, but it would lead us into the alleys of the novel rather than the main highway – which is the account of Gatsby and his dream and some kind of moral evaluation of that dream. At the end Nick makes the point that all of them, including Tom, came from the Midwest, and it may be that Nick's morality extends much more widely into society. He represents normal, decent reaction, particularly in his undertaking to stand by Gatsby throughout the funeral and, really beyond that, to his memory. Perhaps, too, his final rejection of the East represents a rejection of its standards, its superficial, amoral, materialistic life.

Nick makes it clear that he dislikes Tom, but he is not so extreme as to refuse to shake hands with him, though he knows that Tom caused Gatsby's death. This may indicate a capacity for compromise, but it also shows Nick's essential tolerance, a tolerance that paves the way for his understanding of, and later his sympathy for, Gatsby. He has his little bit of 'golden' life when he draws Jordan's head down on to his shoulder; his sympathies are readily engaged; he is considerate but on occasions forthright, as when he gets Gatsby back in the room with Daisy on that wet afternoon. He is thoughtful, and there are moments when he expresses what can only be called wisdom. And this leads us to the final brief phase of analysis – there is little doubt that Nick is Fitzgerald's mouthpiece – the balance, the compassion, the refusal to judge in the conventional way: all these are the characteristics of the omniscient author loosely disguised as the morally committed observer of events.

Daisy

Her face was sad and lovely with bright things in it, bright eyes and a bright passionate mouth, but there was an excitement in her voice that men who had cared for her found difficult to forget.

Daisy is a difficult character, a woman who has married wealth and, equally important, position, and who, though obviously unhappy, cannot do without either. The belle of Louisville, courted by young officers and the centre of attention, she falls in love with the attractive Jay Gatsby. They have an understanding, but Daisy finds the wait irksome and succumbs to the temptation to marry Tom Buchanan – obviously she has never seen wealth equal to his. On the eve of her wedding, her love for Gatsby reasserts itself: she clutches his letter – no one sees what is in it – and she gets very drunk. Sobered up for the next day, she goes through with her wedding and transfers her frustrated love to her husband. For a while she is happy and then, with the birth of her child, knows of Tom's casual infidelity and becomes progressively more bitter. She realizes that she has married not merely a bore, but a man of coarse insensitivity as well; so she has recourse to a kind of flippancy, talking of her 'white girlhood' in deliberate satire of her husband's colour prejudice. She flirts at a superficial level with her cousin Nick, revealing as she does so a good sense of humour, a kind of wit and fun far in advance of her brooding and intractable husband. Platitude though it may be, Daisy lives in a man's world, a beautiful golden girl (Nick's words) in a palace. The knowledge of Gatsby, the nature of his love, plus the contemplation of her selfish husband, and doubtless his supposedly secret life, give her a feeling of elation; whether it is anything more than being the focus of attention again it would be hard to say.

But Daisy does not compromise: she does her utmost to avoid a scene, urges them all to New York, and so precipitates the crisis that will lead inexorably to tragedy. She cannot bring herself to say that she has never loved Tom; and though she asserts that she loves Gatsby, the longer the scene drags on, the nearer they get to returning home, the less convincing she sounds. Daisy fades from the action; reasoned with by a strong and demanding husband she fails to register the existence of Gatsby as an individual, and gives him no signal to comfort his lonely vigil in the bushes. She has capitulated to the demands of the clan; the rich stick together in their riches, the golden girl goes on her travels again.

Daisy asks at one point what will they do for the next thirty years, all too aware of the *ennui* and frustration that is, and will be, her lot. But to be entangled with a bootlegger! Better to stick with a husband who merely smashes women's noses, or directs a murderer to his victim. There is an area of critical opinion which finds Daisy somewhat shallow, and perhaps this accounts for the presentation of her character in the film; in fact she is not so much shallow as a victim of her particular society, of a set-up which reduced the woman by limiting her place to either that of an expensive ornament or the mistress from a lower social class. Daisy has a passionate mouth but there is no evidence of the passion, the vitality, that inform Myrtle: she is of the earth, earthy; whereas Daisy is all flowers, perfume, talc, with a voice that sings, as Gatsby rightly says, of money. Daisy is romantic enough to weep into Gatsby's shirts, but perhaps their cost has something to do with the sentiment behind the tears.

Jordan Baker

She was a slender, small-breasted girl, with an erect carriage, which she accentuated by throwing her body backward at the shoulders like a young cadet. Her grey sun-strained eyes looked back at me with polite reciprocal curiosity out of a wan, charming, discontented face.

It is Lionel Trilling who finds something 'homosexual' in Jordan, but there is little evidence of this. Jordan enjoys a gossip, informing Nick about Tom's woman and the phone call; she is in training, and goes to bed early in order to be ready for the tournament at Westchester. Nick remembers that she has cheated at a previous game, and that there was some publicity in the papers, ending with a caddy retracting his statement. He believes that this is why Jordan keeps things on a superficial level; but Jordan gets caught up in Gatsby's confidences and uses this to get closer to Nick. In a sense she must, since Gatsby has asked her to get Nick to arrange the meeting with Daisy. But she tells Nick that she likes him and later, when they are both fully involved in the Gatsby-Daisy-Tom exchanges, she is somewhat annoyed when Nick does not stay with her. Prior to that Nick has given her some encouragement:

Her wan, scornful mouth smiled, and so I drew her up again closer, this time to my face. (p. 87)

Jordan's mood on the afternoon trip to New York is unlike anything we have seen before, for she speaks of New York as being 'sensuous' (the word upsets Tom) and this really links with her later wish to have Nick stay with her. The next day she telephones him, but he is so caught up with the Gatsby crisis that he doesn't know which of them hangs up on the other. Before that Jordan has made it quite clear that she wants to see Nick; but when they meet after the tragedy, though Nick acknowledges that he is 'half in love with her and tremendously sorry', she tells him that he was a 'bad driver', just as she is. Jordan means that she has misjudged him, and pretends that she is engaged to another man. She is incapable of the involvement that Nick shows in the Gatsby-Daisy affair, but we remember that she too has come from the Midwest, and that she has 'to keep that cool, insolent smile turned to the world and yet satisfy the demands of her hard, jaunty body'.

Other characters

Myrtle registers very positively with us, mainly because of the vivid way in which she is described by Nick, and because her animal warmth contrasts so markedly with the well-powdered indolence of Jordan and Daisy at rest. She is essentially commonplace and down-to-earth, wanting her lover to buy her things ('They're nice to have – a dog') and behaving loudly, stridently, once the 'party' gets under way. Undoubtedly she is making demands on Tom for a divorce, and she has a kind of repressed spirit that rises with the alcohol she has consumed, so that she steps across the class-barrier by shouting the name 'Daisy', and gets her nose broken for her pains. She can be violent and obscene herself, and she is certainly ignorant; it is fairly clear that Tom prefers them this way – they make no demands on his social position – yet there is a curious parallel between Myrtle and Daisy. Both are, up to a point, imprisoned: Daisy is trapped in her palace at East Egg and Myrtle is trapped in the room over the garage. When she makes a break for freedom, after a vicious scene with her husband, the 'death car' rips her open; it is the final stroke of irony that it is Daisy who is driving the car.

Wilson, 'a blond, spiritless man, anaemic and faintly handsome', runs his car business, and is dependent on buying and selling to survive. Significantly, the couple are childless, and Wilson is a gullible man, thinking Myrtle goes to New York to relieve the boredom of the ash-heaps for a few days with her sister. She does, but not innocently. Wilson finds the dog lead, cross-questions her and, in a kind of medieval way, imprisons her. Following the tragedy, his broken hysteria gradually crystallizes into a mystical-religious association with Dr T. J. Eckleburg: Myrtle could not have fooled God, he argues, and there looking down on him *is* God. The result, after Michaelis has left him, is that he goes in search of the driver of the yellow car, initially believing it to be Tom, but finding from the latter that it is Gatsby. Deranged, yes; but Wilson too is the victim of a society that lives to extremes.

Wolfshiem is at first sight caricature, his every inflexion carrying the effect of the smooth, crooked, semi-ignorant but sharp Jew depicted on stage. The man who made Gatsby is a little more than this, his sentimentality and his caution equally mixed. He presents the underworld at the back of material success, the gambler who 'bends' things his way and whose general concerns are covered. He speaks and writes in clichés, for there is no reality in his life that is not dictated by subterfuge, and he sees everything as a 'gonnegtion', initially thinking that Nick has been introduced to him for 'business' reasons. The other characters are slight, more the capturing of a particular mannerism or the reactions to a particular situation than anything else.

McKee and his wife are seen through the smoky and alcoholic haze of Nick's reactions. *Catherine*, too, is seen in the same way, though she is a gossip rather than the beauty her elder sister claims her to be. Fitzgerald is adept at recording moments or incidents: the drunken man with his obstinacy over the crippled car, the *Jewess* who denies Nick entry to Wolfshiem, *Owl-eyes*, *Klipspringer* – all these are real and *seen*. And in terms of minor characterization, this is Fitzgerald's salient quality – the ability to make his people register visually with the reader.

Style and its effects

The Great Gatsby is written in lucid, stringent prose, at once resilient and muscular, yet its metaphorical content is insistent, and its symbolic emphases are part of its universal appeal and significance. There are strong associations with T. S. Eliot's *The Waste Land*, a parallel partly explored by Lionel Trilling in *The Liberal Imagination*; perhaps we should stress not only the ash-heaps of the novel but also the nature of the writing itself, which is spare, never lush, always perspicacious, so that nothing is wasted, nothing lost or forsaken. Strangely, the style stands in contrast to the content: the style is vibrant with life, the story surfeited with death. One is reminded of Cyril Connolly's famous summary of Scott Fitzgerald – 'His style sings of hope, his message is despair.'

There are no innovatory spasms in *The Great Gatsby*; we know from his letters and published statements that Scott Fitzgerald admired Joyce, but the narrative art of the novel would not cause a ripple in the stream of consciousness. There is no post-Laurentian sexuality of explicit or mystical poetic fervour, no mind-shifting, time-moving intensity of experience as intellectualized by Virginia Woolf. In fact, the tone of the narrator has something in common with that of Jane Eyre or Esther Summerson in the *confiding* of a personal experience that is to be shared with the reader. It is an intimate tone, one infinitely capable, in *The Great Gatsby*, of humanizing a bootlegger over 170 pages of sympathetic appraisal (just as Jane's 'Reader, I married him' tames and domesticates Rochester from the autocratic, womanizing, obstinate bore we might otherwise have found him to be).

The device of the autobiographical narrator, a commonplace of fiction, is used by Scott Fitzgerald to establish perspective, to direct the reader's responses, to encourage him to see what the narrator sees, judge as he judges. Nick's presence at the funeral, his 'You're worth the whole damn bunch put together', is the moral currency of the novel, for the big spenders have all gone, disappeared, like Gatsby's money and Gatsby's liquor. The device sets up interesting resonances in the reader's mind – is there something wrong with Nick, who has not fully escaped from the situation back home? What is there in him that makes him so wary of Jordan Baker, for he feels half in love and angry when he says goodbye to her after the tragedy? Nick *is* interesting, and his superb nostalgic recall of returning from school at Christmas, the balancing past of the last chapter, gives us his own intimacy of identity as well as Gatsby's; his moral counterpoise provides the perspective from which to view both Gatsby and his society.

The language is tight but malleable, economical yet with moments of unexpected beauty or wisdom. It is metaphorical in a rich sense, conveying atmosphere intensely on some occasions, reality on others – as in the heat of the Plaza suite and the account of Myrtle's death. At times the language is casual: thus, the people who 'over-populated' Gatsby's lawn 'came and went like moths among the whispering and the champagne and the stars', but Gatsby's station-wagon 'scampered like a brisk yellow bug to meet all trains'. Although the characters of *The Great Gatsby* may have largely forgotten nature, we are never far from it, and one of the expansive effects of the imagery is seen through the 'flower' associations with Daisy, which encompass her and are, in effect, a symbol for her and her. It goes without saying that Daisy and Myrtle are the names of flowers (the first of insipid scent, the latter much more pungent), but I think we can go back to the poignant song of an earlier period to show the depths at which Fitzgerald worked to set up associations in the reader's mind:

Daisy, Daisy,
Give me your answer do;
I'm half crazy,
All for the love of you.
It won't be a stylish marriage,
I can't afford a carriage . . .

But ultimately Gatsby *can* afford one, and the car motif is integral to the tragedy of the novel. All is ephemeral; flowers, like dreams, disappear. Gatsby can send over a greenhouse, to use Nick's word, on the afternoon that Daisy comes to tea; but though his dream has come to life, the hothouse blooms will not survive for long – just as Daisy will not survive the reality of another past. The irony is that a dream, with its intangible quality, can live in its own element, but reality brings change and, ultimately, death.

Flowers, names, these are but two of the associations given wider significance because of the moral resonance that permeates

Fitzgerald's writing. He also uses time and place and their associations: thus Nick, at the beginning of his story, looking back over two years before the unwinding of his experiences with Gatsby, remembers that, 'I wanted the world to be in uniform and at a sort of moral attention forever.' This is a post-war (World War I) image, but Nick's moral awareness is very much part of the tone of the novel. When he first comes to West Egg he thinks of himself as 'a pathfinder, an original settler', the language and ideals and experiences of his forbears being deliberately used to define his own reactions and at the same time to give us, in passing, a taste of history. For *The Great Gatsby* is fundamentally an American novel about American society, the American way of life, and an ironical commentary on the American dream: but it is about the past too, about the pathfinders who made a continent and whose dreams, ambitions, work, made the society that is portrayed in this novel.

The language of *The Great Gatsby* is refined to the point of most vividly evocative expression. Thus Long Island is 'slender riotous', while Long Island Sound is 'a great wet barnyard'; Gatsby's house, first seen, has 'a tower on one side, spanking new under a thin beard of raw ivy'. These quotations may serve as an immediate indication of the variety of metaphorical usage employed in the novel. Consider, too, the effectiveness of the following running personification that is somehow more real than people and, as it proves here, more durable:

The lawn started at the beach and ran toward the front door for a quarter of a mile, jumping over sundials and brick walks and burning gardens – finally when it reached the house drifting up the side in bright vines as though from the momentum of its run. (p. 12)

Here is light and movement, set against the artificiality of the interior with its 'frosted wedding-cake of the ceiling' and 'wine-coloured rug'. In *The Great Gatsby* one of the functions of metaphor is to 'place' society and people on the one hand and to symbolize either the state of society or a personal state on the other. The quality of the symbolic writing is very apparent in this novel: the opening of Chapter II is more than significant – it establishes the contrast, the permanent contrast, between the rich and the poor, and provides the microcosmic intention and intensity of the book. Here nature is present, but only in a distorted analogy of growth:

This is a valley of ashes – a fantastic farm where ashes grow like wheat into ridges and hills and grotesque gardens; where ashes take the forms of houses and chimneys and rising smoke and, finally, with a transcendent effort, of ash-grey men, who move dimly and already crumbling through the powdery air ... above the grey land and the spasms of bleak dust which drift endlessly over it, you perceive, after a moment, the eyes of Dr T. J. Eckleburg. (p. 26)

This is the valley of the shadow of death, given a modern habitation and a name; man reduced, dominated by his environment and contaminated too, contrasting with the 'white palaces' of East Egg, while in the action of the novel itself the grey men are perhaps epitomized by Wilson. Out of this land of desolation comes death – of Gatsby, of Myrtle, of Wilson – and the moral death of being Tom and Daisy: 'they smashed up things and creatures and then retreated back into their money or their vast carelessness, or whatever it was that kept them together, and let other people clean up the mess they had made' (p. 170).

Ashes are the waste land, a land 'grown by man', and it is an additional comment that Dr Eckleburg, who cannot see, remains as a relic of a 'dead' past that included the 'wild wag of an oculist' who made him. He becomes Wilson's God, the symbol of a loss of spiritual and moral direction, and the symbolism rubs off on to Wilson, who loses all direction except that which points him towards the wrong man. The Tiresias of T. S. Eliot's *The Waste Land* is blind too, but he has the gift of prophecy and of suffering, in himself, all experience. But the sightless Dr Eckleburg has lordship over the landscape – with the sightless, sterile look of his 'paintless days'. And the comment that informs his presence is that society also is sterile, in the spiritual sense at least. This important integral symbol has a strong unifying function in the context of the novel. For the sterility of the rich is powerfully stressed, and Wilson's lack of success in material and sexual terms is balanced by the frenetic parties of noncommunication at Gatsby's; the cheating of Jordan Baker; the decadent fixing of Wolfshiem.

Physical and spiritual waste and death, sightless mirroring, all these reflect not merely the twenties but our own time. The 'holocaust' when Wilson's body is found anticipates the wider one, of Hiroshima and beyond, where the ash-heaps are replaced by the radioactive dust that spreads far away from the confines of a lost suburbia. Symbolic representation is endemic to the Fitzgerald method, and perhaps we should note by way of contrast a somewhat different emphasis. On the afternoon when Daisy comes to tea she, Nick and Gatsby go over Gatsby's mansion. Finally they arrive in Gatsby's bedroom after a showy tour of the house and grounds:

He took out a pile of shirts and began throwing them, one by one, before us, shirts of sheer linen and thick silk and fine flannel, which lost their folds as they fell and covered the table in many coloured disarray. While we admired he brought more and the soft rich heap mounted higher – shirts with stripes and scrolls and plaids in coral and apple-green and lavender and faint orange, with monograms of indian blue. (p. 89)

The literary reader will remember two things here: firstly, Fitzgerald's saturation in poetry, his own lifelong habit of writing verse and the fact that *This Side of Paradise* (1920) contains many echoes of Romantic and Swinburnian effects and images. Secondly, the novel on which Fitzgerald laboured so long and which he valued so highly was called *Tender is the Night* (1934). The title is taken from Keats's ode, 'To a Nightingale', but even here in *The Great Gatsby* the Keatsian reverberations are strong, sure and symbolic. The immediate connection of the 'shirt' quotation is with 'The Eve of St Agnes', that romantic legend of virginal fulfilment. In Keats's poem, Porphyro, 'on fire for Madeline', enters the chamber where she is sleeping and sets before her delicious 'dainties' calculated to move her from her dream into the reality of love:

And still she slept an azure-lidded sleep,
In blanched linen, smooth and lavender'd,
While he from forth the closet brought a heap
Of candied apple, quince, and plum, and gourd;
With jellies soother than the creamy curd,
And lucent syrops, tinct with cinnamon;
Manna and dates, in argosy transferr'd
From Fez; and spiced dainties, every one,
From silken Samarcand to cedar'd Lebanon. (Stanza 30)

When she wakes, Madeline, uncertain of what is happening, weeps; Daisy cries 'stormily' into the shirts. Here Fitzgerald quite deliberately, quite consciously, transmutes the legend and its literary associations with superb irony to the situation of his hero. Gatsby puts before Daisy all his riches; Porphyro courts Madeline with riches according to the legend, just as the already dying Keats placed his rich talents at the feet of a scarcely comprehending Fanny Brawne.

Gatsby has observed the rules of his society and is showing Daisy ('Her voice is full of money,' he tells Nick) that he possesses more than her husband – the shirts symbolizing his wealth and, in their texture, the beauty of his dream. But there is a deeper association than this, for though we know that Daisy and Gatsby made physical love those years ago, there is still something virginal, legendary about Gatsby and the needs of his dream; he wants Daisy to say that she never loved Tom; he wants to marry Daisy from her home in Louisville, as if the past can be eliminated and everything made pure again. Keats's poem is a romantic narrative of romantic love, Fitzgerald's scene a poignantly ironic appraisal of romantic love doomed to die in a society which has a measure for superficiality but not sincerity. Again, the example serves to point the range of extensions from the text: in terms of literary, social, moral and spiritual awareness Fitzgerald is one of the great writers of this century.

There are many other qualities in his writing. Fitzgerald wrote for the theatre, and throughout his stories too there is a fine ear for dialogue that is virtually faultless. The racial and local intonations of Wolfshiem are a case in point:

'He has to telephone,' said Mr. Wolfshiem, following him with his eyes. 'Fine fellow, isn't he? Handsome to look at and a perfect gentleman.'
  'Yes.'
  'He's an Oggsford man.'
  'Oh!'
  'He went to Oggsford College in England. You know Oggsford College?' (p.70)

The truth of hearing (listen to what is said at the first Gatsby party, particularly by the drunken man whose car is 'shorn' of a wheel), is allied to the truth of seeing and feeling in terms of physical observation and sensation. Thus of Myrtle, Nick observes that 'there was an immediately perceptible vitality about her as if the nerves of her body were continually smouldering' (p. 28). Seeing one thing in terms of another is a constant in Fitzgerald's writing, and is part of the metaphorical usage glanced at earlier; and we note that 'the cab stopped at one slice in a long white cake of apartment houses' (p. 31).

This kind of observation has in it on occasion a fine, unusual sense of perspective, and we are able to view Myrtle with a curious intensity of focus, for 'as she expanded the room grew smaller around her, until she seemed to be revolving on a noisy, creaking pivot through the smoky air' (p. 33). Fitzgerald's ear repeats easily the clichés of the time: 'I lay down and cried to beat the band all afternoon ... Tom's the first sweetie she ever had' (p. 37). He is the master too of the sudden, surprise, economical statement, for example violence erupting, the few words recording exactly the speed, the time such an action takes – 'Making a short deft movement, Tom Buchanan broke her nose with his open hand.' (p. 39) The ironic tone, of course, permeates *The Great Gatsby*, for the whole concept is fundamentally an ironic one – the dream of a man who has resorted to criminal activity in order to give himself a chance with the woman of whom he has never ceased to dream. The bread-and-butter irony of the novel, however, is insistent. Speaking of Tom Buchanan, Nick observes that he is to be found 'wherever people played polo and were rich together', while at one of the parties Nick is ironic at his own expense:

I was enjoying myself now. I had taken two finger-bowls of champagne, and the scene had changed before my eyes into something significant, elemental, and profound. (p 48)

But here Fitzgerald is laughing at himself too, with the self-conscious awareness of the writer gathering the ephemeral and the superficial into the note-book of experience.

Fitzgerald does not spare his own time: mocking the pretentiousness of 'Vladimir Tostoff's Jazz History of the World' (p. 51); or more seriously the craze for speed epitomized in Myrtle's death or when Jordan 'passed so close to some workmen that our fender flicked a button on one man's coat'. Again the rich–poor contrast is apparent, together with a fine sense of detail, which unifies the theme. Perhaps the high-water-mark of the ironic tone is to be found at the beginning of Chapter 4, when Fitzgerald creates for Gatsby his own mythology, peopling his parties with a gratuitously satirical list of 'those who accepted Gatsby's hospitality and paid him the subtle tribute of knowing nothing whatever about him'. The irony is extended, of course, by the fact that none of them attends his funeral. Fitzgerald produces a list which includes the Leeches, the Willie Voltaires, a 'whole clan named Blackbuck', Clarence Endive, S. P. Whitebait and G. Earl Muldoon, 'brother to that Muldoon who afterwards strangled his wife'. On one level, the level of sheer ingenuity, the ripple of names on the tongue is sheer humour – we are in the world of Dickens, of Trollope, of P. G. Wodehouse, of names like Micawber, Glencora McGlusky and Catsmeat Potter-Pirbright.

But on another level the list is mock-heroic, an imitation Homeric list of gods and goddesses, or a Miltonic list of angels and archangels. It implies that the story of Gatsby is mock-epic, for these people are only of heroic stature in the passing world of crookedness or high finance. Read the list carefully and you will note the incidence of violence and violent death – another comment on life in America in the early twenties.

Dress, too, comes in for a passing focus in relation to the times. Gatsby at one stage wears a 'caramel-coloured suit' and when Nick sees him for the last time he refers to his 'gorgeous pink rag of a suit'. These simple statements are an index to the flashiness, the superficial and the temporary as distinct from the permanent. No amount of self-advertising, and, in Gatsby's case, no compensatory number of 'old sports' can be any substitute for integrity.

Technically the use of retrospect is another interesting device. The whole of the narrative is set in the past – Nick is two years away from the experience – and interspersed in it there are further returns to the past, for example, where Jordan Baker fills in Gatsby's and Daisy's meetings. Immediately after this another Fitzgerald technique is apparent – the almost casual use of song to reiterate a theme. The 'Sheik of Araby' was a popular song of the time, and if you look at the verse here you will see that it links with the 'Eve of St Agnes' theme and with the Gatsby dream. It is appropriate too in the high romantic sense, for the period of the novel and the publication of Gatsby (setting 1922, publication 1925) is the period of the sheik of the silent screen, Rudolph Valentino. The use of this popular song is thus a further underlining of the romantic element in the novel.

Fitzgerald uses song to convey the flavour of the time, but even more effective is his ability to convey a particular atmosphere, like rain or heat, again used as contrast. When Daisy comes to tea it is a very wet day where 'occasional thin drips swarm like dew' and the windows are described as 'bleared'. An even more telling description is when Nick is on his way to have lunch with Jordan, Tom, Gatsby and Daisy. He is on the train, and the broiling hot day, which is to destroy the romantic dream, has a subtle anticipation in Nick's ironic thoughts:

My commutation ticket came back to me with a dark stain from his hand. That anyone should care in this heat whose flushed lips he kissed, whose head made damp the pyjama pocket over his heart! (p. 110)

This is a very deliberate foretaste; with the day, so to speak, taking over destiny. For later the heat is to drive Daisy into suggesting the drive to New York, which sets into motion the fatal sequence of coincidences that breaks all dreams.

These are a few indications of the main stylistic devices in *The Great Gatsby*. They have a resonant morality about them: from the narrative tone to the metaphorical vivacity; from dialogue to symbol; through social and literary associations. The unifying element of *The Great Gatsby* is the author's serious and abiding concern for the human situation of his own time, and indeed for all time.

His style *makes* Fitzgerald the writer he is — refined, ironic, wise, compassionate, prophetic — and his literary manners have the impeccable stamp of a breeding his tragic hero spent so much time trying to acquire.

General questions plus questions on related topics for coursework/examinations on other books you may be studying

1 Write an essay on the main aspects of the narrative art in *The Great Gatsby*.

Suggested notes for essay answer:
You might consider the following – make your own plan, but refer to some of these, giving them the importance that you feel each one merits:

(a) The use of the first person narrator – his relationship to the characters – what he learns about himself – his perspectives.

(b) The use of retrospect – refer to two or three incidents to show how effective this is in integrating character.

(c) The style of the novel – vivid descriptions, sense of the period, disillusion, extravagance, moral tone, dialogue.

(d) The way the author gets us interested in particular characters, and the nature of those characters.

(e) The use of techniques not mentioned above – i.e. the unexpected (when Tom breaks Myrtle's nose) and the dramatic (Myrtle's death).

2 Write an appreciation of Fitzgerald's use of contrast in the novel.
3 Compare Daisy and Myrtle as characters, and say whether or not you feel sympathetic to either or both of them, giving reasons for your answer.
4 In what ways do you feel interested in Nick Carraway? Is he as fascinating as the story he tells? Give reasons for your answer.
5 Discuss Fitzgerald's use of symbol in *The Great Gatsby*.
6 By a close analysis of two scenes, show how Fitzgerald is able to create a convincing atmosphere.
7 In what ways is *The Great Gatsby* a moral work? Give reasons for your answer.
8 Do you find Jay Gatsby a likeable character or not? Give reasons for your answer.

9 Write an essay on the effectiveness of Fitzgerald's dialogue in *The Great Gatsby*, quoting by way of illustration.

10 Judging from this novel, what seem to you to be the main characteristics of society in New York and on Long Island at the time?

11 Write a considered appraisal of the characters of Jordan Baker and Meyer Wolfshiem, saying clearly what you think they represent.

12 What aspects of *The Great Gatsby* do you find humorous, and why?

13 Write an essay on the use of *irony* in *The Great Gatsby*.

14 Write an appreciation of any aspect of the novel not mentioned above.

15 Compare *The Great Gatsby* with any other novel of city life, showing clearly where it differs from the other novel you have chosen.

16 What aspects of *The Great Gatsby* do you find romantic, and why?

17 Write an account of a book you have read which is mainly about rich people.

18 In which of the books you have studied is there a sudden tragedy? Describe it, bringing out the quality of the author's writing.

19 Nick is the first-person narrator of the novel. Write about any book you know well which has a first-person narrative.

20 Write about a book you have studied where *deception* is a main theme.

21 Describe any two characters in a novel you have read or a play you have seen who contrast with each other.

Tender is the Night
A note on the Cowley version

Fitzgerald spent about nine years writing, revising and pondering on the sequence of *Tender is the Night*. In 1933 (it was first published in 1934) he claimed to have written 400,000 words and to have 'thrown away three-fourths of it'. Nevertheless, he believed that when people read it they would say 'it's good, good, good'. Generally they didn't, and it sold fewer copies than his earlier novels. He tried, according to Malcolm Cowley, to account for this, and came to consider that perhaps the order of the novel was responsible for its lukewarm reception. Cowley quotes him as saying, 'Its great fault is that the *true* beginning – the young psychiatrist in Switzerland – is tucked away in the middle of the book.' He produced a 'final version', and this was published by Cowley in its straight chronological sequence in 1951. This was used as the standard text by Penguin books from 1955 until 1982. In that year it was issued in its present order by Penguin with an editorial note by Arnold Goldman. This note explains the reasons for reverting to the First Edition of 1934. The interested student should study Goldman's remarks. For this Brodie's Note the Goldman edition has been used, and it is this order which should be studied by any reader of the novel.

Section commentaries, textual notes and revision questions

Book I

I (pp.11–15)

The first paragraph is a superb set-piece of description which economically establishes the location. There are fine turns of phrase ('Deferential palms') and vivid images – the cupolas 'rotted like water lilies'. Colour is omnipresent and the sun-worshippers (money-worshippers too) are given an appropriate metaphor in the 'bright tan prayer-rug of a beach'. The effects of time and change are registered: the setting is a perfect backcloth, the characters of the drama soon appear. There are hints from the description of Rosemary's character, while the atmosphere of the ever-present heat is conveyed through such details as the car which 'cooked on the drive'. Authorial irony, a feature of the style, is seen in the remark that the nannies' gossip is 'as formalized as incantation'. Rosemary is now named and we, like the man with the monocle, are aware of her sexually. Her swimming is described in terms of erotic experience as she embraces and wallows. People are now superimposed on place: there is an atmosphere of decadence and indolence, with hints of violence and living it up to the point of hangover, the 'relic of the previous evening' having her tiara still while 'a discouraged orchid expired from her shoulder'. The word 'expired' is almost definitive of this languid self-indulgence. The reader's attention however is now turned to the other 'characters', the girl with the hard but pitiful face perhaps provoking the greatest interest, though the jockey-capped man is performing for the benefit of others and is enjoying in a straight-faced way his 'esoteric burlesque'. He commands 'the antennae of attention'. That Rosemary herself is a centre of attention is apparent too, for she is a celebrity. The ironic tone runs throughout, embracing the woman who is 'impervious to experience'. The chapter – a segment of the unfolding experience – ends in the middle of a conversational exchange.

like the thrilling flush of children Note the warm domestic image which contrasts so tellingly with this superficial society.

knitting the slow pattern of Victorian England ... i.e. the nannies
symbolize the wealth of their employers.
flotte Fleet.
peignoir Loose dressing-gown.

II (pp.16–20)

This begins with the mystery of the 'plot', subsequently identified as part of the running joke against that budding novelist
McKisco. Note the distinction between this group and the
socially more desirable group (from Rosemary's angle). The
irritability between the McKiscos and the sadness of the man
with the leonine head form a dramatic focus, while the introduction to Abe North prepares us for what is to come. The picture,
ironically drawn, is of Americans at play. Rosemary finds herself
taken up by the man in the jockey-cap, and this first encounter
with Dick Diver shows him organizing his pleasure, and that of
others, the major part of his function in this section of the novel.
He is already protective towards Rosemary, the role he has
played in life with Nicole.

Antheil George Antheil (1900–59) American composer.
like a volcanic island ... Vivid sudden image – and Abe himself is on
the edge of sudden violence in the novel.
He takes a decayed old French aristocrat ... Note the ridiculous
nature of this – heavy irony.

III (pp.20–24)

Rosemary's sudden confession of love for Dick: she is self-
consciously creating the experience. The retrospect (flashback
sequences are a favourite Fitzgerald device – see Book II for this
kind of integration at length) on Mrs Speers does much to
explain Rosemary. The success of 'Daddy's Girl' (note the title
and its significance – it runs throughout the novel) has made this
trip possible. Mrs Speers is still intent on Rosemary's career, as
we see when she urges her to visit Earl Brady, the film producer.
We sense Rosemary's immaturity in her uncertainty about
whether she will stop long. This is followed by a shift of concen-
tration to Nicole: we are aware that there is something strange
about her – 'her lovely face set, controlled, her eyes brave and
watchful'. The drive on the following day emphasizes the

passage of time: the Russian prince's reference gives a wider perspective, but we have the feeling too that the Americans will depart, that time changes everything. This is one of the themes of the novel. Rosemary's romantic, almost dream-like state, is shown by her hoping to meet the Divers and thus alleviate her boredom.

a double sheath of her mother's armor ... An image which indicates Rosemary's toughness.
the clamor of Empire A contrast with the English.
Gausse père ... concierge ... métier Gausse senior ... door-keeper, porter ... position.
hacks Carriages.
Le Temps The Times.
Saturday Evening Post One of the leading American papers.
Ivan the Terrible Ivan IV, Czar of Russia (1530–84).
the lost caviare days i.e. the good old days of wealth and plenty for the Russian aristocrats before the Communist Revolution of 1917.
estaminets French cafés, cottages, selling wine, beer.

IV (pp.24–31)

Dick's sympathetic and outgoing nature is shown, his sensitivity appreciated by the infatuated – determined to be infatuated – Rosemary. The detailed description of Nicole stresses her unusual quality. Rosemary is susceptible – she is quick to change her mind and decide to stay, now that she is 'in' with this socially desirable set. Her passing revelation about having pneumonia is virtually swamped by her response to the social impressiveness of the Divers. This in turn is followed by the comedy of the list of names, which vary in their humour from the obvious to the subtle. Tommy Barban also registers positively with the reader. Rosemary's interest in Dick becomes obvious in an unspoken way to Nicole. The conversation is full of wordplay and humorous innuendo, these Americans at play mocking the British at play. Dick shows his need to experiment, probably as a means of gaining excitement, by inviting the McKiscos to dinner. The group seem to be motivated (indolently) towards the prospect of new experience. This is what passes for life here. The day must be filled: Rosemary feels that Dick is taking care of her (another underlining of 'Daddy's Girl'). Dick clad in 'black lace drawers' lined with 'flesh-colored cloth' is another expression of the need for sensation, here the wish to shock, to produce an effect. Rosemary, having fallen in love with Dick as the focus, now enjoys the prospect. As always, she confides in her mother.

broke down i.e. relaxed.
a Rodinesque intention Derived from Auguste Rodin (1840–1917), the French sculptor.
'They invented it.' A good example of Abe's humour.
garçon ... chasseur Waiter ... footman or page-boy.
Mme. Bonneasse ... Note the list of parody names, similar to the ones in *The Great Gatsby*, and often crudely physical, as here.
wit de quality i.e. Abe's low life humour. 'de quality' is the upper class, one's social superiors.
a pansy's trick i.e. a homosexual joke.

V (pp.31–34)

From the Divers to the film set is almost a natural transition, the society actors to the professionals. Brady is not quite caricature, there is some pathos in Rosemary's awareness of herself as property, and Fitzgerald's ironic cynicism informs the scene. 'Daddy's Girl' continues as an important notation in the action. The dialogue is crisp, direct, superficial, though Rosemary's awareness of herself sexually is becoming more and more apparent. The period atmosphere is conveyed through the movie references: we note too Rosemary's needs – the studio is her reassurance, since she knows that she, mother's girl, rules in that brittle world. The section closes with a death association. Rosemary is being freed to live by her mother, but there is the implication that this superficial life – whether in films or on the Riviera – is a kind of death too.

Gaumont Film company.
First National ... Famous Names of film companies.
Connie Talmadge Celebrated star of silent films.

VI (pp.34–41)

In the first section here style and experience blend – there is a beautiful simplicity about the experience of Nicole in her garden, a kind of physical and spiritual retreat in itself. Even here there are signs of decadence in the 'atrophied and faintly rotten' wheelbarrow. Always there is the emphasis on Nicole's eyes, which are the mirror of the past, her insecurity, her fear. The changes in her are noted, while the squabble in the background cuts across the silence of nature: there is also the effect of colour, the contrasts deftly conveyed. Nicole's character is explored here in precise, economical phrasing, her reticence, her sudden outrushing after the muted period indicating a neurosis which is for the most part contained but which is also sometimes exposed. Dick's passing her here is almost symbolic of their later separation. The megaphone reinforces this suggestion, and her acquiescence to the 'really bad party' is an apathy which contrasts with Dick's craving for sensation. Nicole rightly reads his mood as one of excitement which will be followed inevitably by melancholy. Dick at this stage compels the love and admiration of others, but he knows inside himself the appalling waste. He is polite, considerate, and depends on the affection of others. The seeds of his disintegration are within him. Having contemplated Dick at some length the authorial voice – an important perspective in the novel – restores us to Rosemary's angle.

At the party which follows, the children's song is a moment of innocence and simplicity, though the words carry their own poignant associations. Rosemary, naïve in some ways despite the toughness and conditioning of her career, is taken aback by Dick's mixed choice of guests. There is an unpleasant, significant emphasis on the mercenary but potent Tommy Barban. Rosemary seems rather frightened of him, thinking that her own moral stance is right and that Barban is wrong. She feels that she can do what she wishes with Dick because of her mother's approval. In the chat with Brady – he refuses to play the part of Daddy to this Daddy's girl – Rosemary is always aware of Dick. She is cultivating her obsession.

the soft gleam of piteous doubt . . . An indication of Nicole's mental illness, her uncertainty.

as a general might gaze upon a massacre . . . One of the war associations which run through the text.

she nags it all the time . . . The garden is at once Nicole's obsession and her refuge.

"Au clair de la lune . . . Song plays an important part in the novel – it is an index to a situation. 'By the light of the moon, my friend Pierrot, lend me your pen so that I can write a note. My candle is burnt out, I have no longer any fire, open your door to me for the love of God.' Readers may estimate the effect here.

that he refused the fatherly office Note the irony and remember that Rosemary is 'Daddy's Girl'.

VII (pp.41–6)

Abe North and the idea of sawing up the waiter gives rise to jokey banter, here sick with the craving for sensation. The antics of McKisco are endured by Dick with determined self-discipline: he will not be drawn or exposed. The temperature of the party changes. Rosemary is possessive over her new friends. There is some 'devastating irony' (McKisco's words), and none of it is more expressive than the author's at the expense of Violet McKisco, when he refers to her as 'the wife of an arriviste who had not arrived'.

Abe's failure as a composer is perhaps the reason for his whimsically sick humour. Rosemary feels more and more at home. Cunningly, the perspective shifts, and we see the group isolated in their own world: a pathetic image summarizes their craving, with their longings 'like the faces of poor children at a Christmas tree'. Here, paradoxically, wealth and its associations are equated with human deprivation. After the poetry of the scene, there comes the destructive dialogue between Tommy Barban and McKisco, and this is in turn followed by the high tension of what Mrs McKisco saw that she can't speak about. Tommy Barban, who loves the Divers, puts the brake on what she might say anyway.

an arriviste Ambitious person, one who thrusts forward.
Mrs Burnett's vicious tracts i.e. the highly moral stories of Frances Hodgson-Burnett (1849–1924), who wrote *Little Lord Fauntleroy* and *The Secret Garden*.

VIII (pp.46–8)

This maintains the tension. Dick copes with it, while Rosemary is intent on being alone with him. The dialogue between them is subtly appropriate: Rosemary is determined, Dick drawn to her in spite of himself, or perhaps just playing up to the sensation of being admired, loved – the role he enjoys. Dick's extremes are reflected in his wish that the last of the summer should 'die violently', and this does happen when Rosemary accompanies them as he suggests. Fitzgerald's narrative art is tightly controlled: everything looks forward or relates to everything else. A religious image ('like a chasuble') shows the extent of Rosemary's worship. It is significant though that Dick draws back and returns to the terrace where he 'delivered her' (Rosemary) to Nicole. In the process he has delivered himself from temptation. What did Mrs McKisco see in the bathroom? The tension is finely maintained.

IX (pp.49–52)

Narrative focuses first on the car, then Rosemary's insomnia. Here Fitzgerald employs retrospect to integrate Rosemary. The influence of mummy on mummy's girl is always apparent, for she urges Rosemary to gain experience with Dick ('Wound yourself or him'), while assuring her daughter of her financial security – 'economically you're a boy, not a girl'. Dramatic tension is now injected: Rosemary encounters the weeping Campion (presumably rejected by a possible male lover). It becomes supercharged when she absorbs his news about the absurdity but nevertheless the fact of the duel. Above this sick comedy is the punctuation of the affected speech of the English. Notice how Campion enjoys telling his story: we know now that something Violet McKisco said has infuriated Tommy Barban. Dick's wish that things should end up violently looks like coming true.

an insistent bird achieved an ill-natured triumph . . . The associations are with Keats's *Ode to a Nightingale*, which provides the title of the novel.
coo-coo Mad, strange, silly.

X (pp.53–7)

Retrospect is again employed to fill in the necessary details. There is an effective transition from reported speech to the dramatic immediacy of the incident in dialogue. It is a typical example of an incident getting out of hand, though even this is interlaced with comedy, like Violet McKisco falling asleep after the bromide. The meeting with McKisco is charged with pathos: his acknowledgment that he doesn't want to get too sober is a sad reminder of the ridiculous but potentially tragic situation. The 'aghast laugh' says it all. The revelation that they had a child who died (Daddy's girl?) does much to account for McKisco's behaviour. There is an air of grim farce about the final preparations. It is, and this is obviously deliberate, like a scene in a film.

he called them on it i.e. took them up on it, warned them.

clapped him one Challenged him – by a light slap on the face.

a novel of Pushkin's Pushkin (1799–1837), Russia's greatest poet and writer, his poems being often novels in verse.

XI (pp.57–61)

Although Rosemary resents the suggestion, the idea of McKisco as a 'tragic clown' is somehow appropriate. There is a hint here from Campion that Royal Dumphry has rejected his advances. Typically, Rosemary confides in her mother, who approves her seeing the duel (from a respectable distance, of course). Rosemary's obedience is predictable, while Campion generates almost hysterical excitement at the prospect. The anti-climax is inevitable but orchestrated by Abe's dry humour and the grotesque comedy of the doctor in attendance asking for his money. Note the realism of McKisco's reaction – his initial blarney followed by vomiting. He mentions the universal drunkenness in the war, which Fitzgerald does not let us forget. Campion collapses while Rosemary joyfully anticipates the future on the beach with 'the Divers' whom she still, curiously but understandably perhaps, thinks of as one person. The fact is that they personify the way of life she is intent on experiencing.

'Pardon, Messieurs . . . porte-monnaie chez-lui.' 'Pardon, gentlemen . . . would you settle my account? Naturally it is only for my medical attendance. M. Barban has only a thousand franc note and is unable to settle up, and the other has left his purse with you.'

XII (pp.61–6)

Here we see the Diver group at play again, trying to identify 'repose', which Dick claims that he alone has. The reflexes of the other guests are noted, while Dick continually observes Rosemary. She in her turn notices that he introduces people into their group, and then puts them down ironically. The drinking and the laughter constitute a kind of running decadence, a satirical glance at the various class layers of American life, with Rosemary acting as a catalyst in the group. Meanwhile, she has laid her own plans by getting the print of 'Daddy's Girl'. Personal drama intervenes, for Rosemary overhears the sexual need Nicole has for Dick and his desire for her. Rosemary is deeply moved, though she does not understand what is happening to herself. Nicole's shopping, the natural indulgence of her wealth, is satirically described. The associations with Keats which run throughout the novel from the title onwards are finely integrated here (see note below). Nicole's reference to the hard social ambitions of her mother, seen in the story about Baby, reflects the unscrupulous upward mobility evident in the American way of life. The tensions in this chapter arise from Rosemary thinking all the time of Nicole's assignation with Dick.

a Mayfair party in Hollywood i.e. a superior social gathering.
President Tyler John H. Tyler took office in 1841.
vestiaire Cloak-room.
For her sake trains began their run at Chicago . . . Further evidence of Fitzgerald's indebtedness to Keats – the idea of slave labour with all working to provide for the rich is present in Keats's *Isabella* in the lines beginning 'For them the Ceylon diver held his breath/And went all naked to the hungry shark . . .'

XIII (pp.66–70)

This superb chapter is full of war associations and the effects and characteristics of the post-war mood. We note the irony: Dick has not seen battle service and is showing off for Rosemary's benefit, while Rosemary in her turn is tense with love for him. Dick is in the full flow of war summary, of exaggeration, of associations, of sentiment and romance too despite his denials. Rosemary is moved, but this is largely because Dick has created this mood of emotional response in her. The terrible anonymity of death is captured in the incident of the girl with the wreath. Fitzgerald employs throwaway irony ('altogether it had been a watery day'). The atmosphere of period and place is captured here, as so often in Fitzgerald, through popular song in 'Yes, We Have No Bananas'. The conclusion of this chapter stresses, in terrifying finality, the widespread anonymity of death. Also, there is the revelation about Dick: he has mastered this subject – this relic of the battlefield of the Great War – in the same way that he has master-minded his own parties, but perhaps not his own career.

Thiepval Scene of terrible battle casualties in the Great War.
Marne Major battle in the war.

General Grant ... Petersburg Grant was the great Northern General in the American Civil War (1861–65), later President.

Lewis Caroll The pseudonym of Charles Dodgson, who wrote *Alice's Adventures in Wonderland* (1865).

Jules Verne (1828–1905). French writer of science fiction (*Twenty Thousand Leagues Under the Sea*).

Undine The female water spirit, subject of a novel by De La Motte Fouque.

D. H. Lawrence Celebrated contemporary of Scott Fitzgerald's, author of *Sons and Lovers* and *Lady Chatterley's Lover*.

Silver cord ... golden bowl The whole passage is a warning to the young and confident that death comes to all. See Ecclesiastes xii,l.

'Yes, We Have No Bananas' Another popular, somewhat nonsensical song of the period, typical of the craving for lightheartedness.

of Württembergers ... The list comprises the mixed war dead of both sides.

XIV (pp.70–73)

In Paris Nicole separates from them, much to Rosemary's relief, since she is rather afraid of her. Rosemary herself gets caught up in the group's drinking (it is already apparent that Abe North is an alcoholic), for she feels that this will bring her closer to Dick. She is obviously contriving to seduce him. But note that parallels and contrasts are being developed – Abe and Dick are both failures, for we feel that Dick will never complete his medical treatise. There are hints that Mary North loves Dick and that she will survive whatever happens.

a part of the equipment for what she had to do A factual way of indicating that she is intent on sexual experience with Dick.

XV (pp.73–7)

Dick and Rosemary in the taxi, with the reader aware of the Daddy's girl associations, Dick even calling her a 'lovely child'. He is used to this kind of language. Yet he is 'chilled by the innocence of her kiss', and manages to recover his paternal attitude when they get to her room. Authorial irony plays over her wish to be taken by Dick. As she utters her needs in stereotyped phrases, the 'role' she is playing becomes one of her greatest, and she acquires the passion to go with it. Dick paternalistically points out all the disadvantages and his own love for Nicole, but as Rosemary weeps he finds himself – rare for him – at a loss as to what to do. Even the word 'forlorn' here reminds the alert reader of the key word in the last verse of Keats's *Ode to a Nightingale*, with its insistence on beauty and death. It is significant however that Rosemary only sniffles a little when Dick has gone: she ploughs through her mechanistic ritual of brushing her hair – after all, it is one of the important parts of herself as 'property'.

the dark cave of the taxi Another vividly evocative metaphor.
chilled by the innocence . . . Rosemary has been concentrating on her career so much that she has little sexual experience. But remember Collis Clay's story which so haunts Dick.
The night had drawn the color from her face . . . i.e. it is anything but tender – an ironic reference to the title of the novel.

XVI (pp.77–82)

Afterwards Rosemary's reaction is to play down what has happened. This is human in view of her rejection, though she is very jealous of Nicole. She is aware of the social differences between them as each reveals to the other a segment of the past. But Dick had fallen in love with her: we may feel that this is the beginning of his disintegration. There is meanwhile some passing irony at the expense of Collis Clay, and an equally brief comment on the changes in Rosemary herself. Watching 'Daddy's Girl' brings Rosemary and Dick into physical proximity, but we sense that Nicole is aware of their attraction to each other. A brilliant paragraph sends up the sentiment on which Rosemary's career has been reared, and it also sends up the cinema-going public who are moved by the synthetic representation which appeals to the emotional and rejects the rational in each of us. The 'father complex' reference underlines Fitzgerald's structural strategy: Dick is himself to stand as father to Rosemary in a sense, just as he has so stood to the emotionally maimed Nicole. Rosemary's trump card – her arranging a screen test for Dick – nominally flops, but in fact he is flattered and moved. There is some light comedy in the presence of Collis Clay as obstruction to Dick and Rosemary being alone.

tanagra From the town of Tanagra in Ancient Greece famous for its terracotta work.

'itty-bitty bravekins... Sentimental baby talk to indicate the sentimentality which adults indulge when young girls are involved. Fitzgerald is sending up the contemporary vogue for brave little girls, seen, for instance, in films starring Shirley Temple.

a Duncan Phyfe dining-room. Duncan Phyfe (1768–1854) American cabinet-maker.

a father complex so apparent... Very ironic, in view of Dick's marriage to Nicole and the difference in age between himself and Rosemary.

XVII (pp.82–7)

The scene to which Dick conducts Rosemary is artificial, made so by the air of decadence which is apparent. The people are a synthetic set on what appears to Rosemary to be a set. There is an atmosphere which reflects impersonality – the English and the Americans are alternately lethargic or neurotically alive. It is as if Dick is deliberately holding up the mirror of this group for Rosemary. The latter is scared. The three young women are predatory, almost like a perverted chorus, the image of flowers being superseded by the deadly image of cobras. Their language, like the place and the company, is poisoned. Rosemary realizes that the talk she hears is about the Divers, that it has currents of criticism in it, and that while this is going on she is being chatted up by her lesbian companion. The transition to the outside world finds Rosemary weeping, while Dick confesses his love after the craving which she made him show her earlier. Fitzgerald is ironic about the illusions that each is nursing, though Dick insists that his love will change nothing. This is blind, decadent, but at least we understand his motivation. Dick is now defensive, half explaining what is wrong with Nicole but saying that she isn't strong. Rosemary continues starry-eyed over Dick (the 'curator of richly incrusted happiness') but handles the situation well, only pricked by the conscience of not missing her mother.

Cardinal de Retz's palace (1614–79). French Churchman.

Louisa M. Alcott (1832–88), American authoress of a number of books, the most celebrated being *Little Women*.

Madame de Ségur (1799–1874). Wrote stories for the young.

The Frankenstein The monster – based on the creation by the hero (Frankenstein) of a monster, from Mary Shelley's novel of that name (1818).

XVIII (pp.88–91)

The party craving for sensation is exemplified in this sequence. The car is the symbol of wealth, of what is fabulous and exciting in this determined passing of time in the pursuit of what appears to be happiness. Their companions are types and names, the whirling experience stimulated by drink, the practical jokes showing the lack of substance behind the frenzied activity. There is a neat ironic twist in Nicole saying (of Rosemary) that she and Dick feel 'responsible to her mother'. The 'wild party' converts the morning into the night before: the symbol of the horse-chestnut tree, in full bloom, is identified by Rosemary with herself. Strangely, the blossom of life is to wither for all of them in this fated group, Rosemary excepted.

'Major Hengest and Mr Horsa' Brothers, the first died 488, the second 455; they virtually founded Kent and began the Anglo-Saxon conquest of England.

General Pershing The American General who commanded his country's forces in the First World War.

a Goldberg cartoon Ruben Lucius Goldberg (1883–1970), cartoonist of grotesque devices.

XIX (pp.91–8)

Abe in isolation, hungover, but watching, waiting perhaps, we feel, for Nicole. When she arrives, and talks too fast, we feel the tension between them and also Abe's self-knowledge about how he has wasted himself. He is nervous and irritable, and, although there is friction between them, he loves Nicole. The tall girl now becomes the focus of attention – and tension – particularly when she snubs Nicole. With the arrival of Rosemary and Mary North we feel a strange symbolic atmosphere, almost as if the women are the three Marys attending a grotesque, broken Christ, here with the death-wish upon him. Dick transforms everything when he arrives. All three women are in love with him, and the contrast with Abe is immediate. The scene at the station with the numbers of wealthy Americans invites the usual Fitzgerald irony, but the moment becomes dramatic with death as the tall girl shoots the man and confusion follows. Dick and the women are caught up in it. Note that the gendarmes are 'distraught' while the girl is 'firm and pale', almost a reversal of what we should expect. There is a touch of the grotesque in the man being shot through his identity card. Dick is chivalric about Maria Wallis, intent on involving himself and showing off before Rosemary. There is a sharpness of observation in the interaction between Rosemary and Dick afterwards. He is undermined by Rosemary's constant mention of her mother, and above all by the fact that Rosemary is now really in control of their affair. Another war image, this time of shell fragments, is used to express the horror of what has happened.

the Crystal Palace The magnificent building made of iron and glass designed by Sir Joseph Paxton for the Great Exhibition in London (1851).

the three women sprang like monkeys with cries of relief The image is an uneasy but ironic one – almost a parody of the three Marys attendant on Christ.

Diaghileff (1872–1929), the Russian impresario who founded the Russian ballet company (1909) which led to a revival of the ballet in the main European centres.

XX (pp.98–104)

There is an interesting reaction when Dick and Nicole are left together, as she evaluates Dick – he has always needed people, always needed to pick them up and make use of them. But after Nicole has gone Dick's feelings for Rosemary are exposed by Collis Clay's story of her on the train with the boy. Dick is made jealous by this snippet of information about Rosemary's past: the phrase repeated in his consciousness is indicative of his anguish. The writing of the cheque and the thumbing through the letters shows Dick mechanically keeping himself occupied, but the last letter is for Rosemary and this sets off once more his emotional obsession. Outwardly he is engaged in his usual game with people, making himself a focus of interest. Throughout this sequence we are aware of money; Dick has bribed ('purchased') the doorman but he is thrown into insecurity by the effect Rosemary has produced on him. The shirts in the window symbolize the many dead in the war, and contribute by this association to increasing Dick's sense of melancholy in this miserable neighbourhood. Yet he feels a strange compulsion to be where he is.

'**worked over**' i.e. used for their companionship.

Grand Guignol The theatre in Montmartre specializing in sensational plays.

staked to a year in Milan i.e. paid for his training (as an opera singer).

beyed Southern pronunciation of 'bird'.

Do you mind if I pull down the curtain? The phrase repeats itself in Dick's consciousness, the beginning of his jealousy over Rosemary.

Tarkington's adolescents Booth Tarkington (1869–1946), American novelist, his major sequence describing the adventures of a boy and his companions.

Papeterie ... Pâtisserie ... Solde ... Réclame Bookshop, stationers ... cake-shop ... surplus stock ... advertising.

Constance Talmadge See note on page 59.

Déjeuner du Soleil Lunch in the Sun.

Vêtements Ecclésiastiques Clerical robes.

Déclaration de Décès Death registration.

Pompes Funèbres Funerals.

XXI (pp.104–8)

He is, however, 'involved in human contact' with the thin American – another war-relic. The latter has come down in the world – is he an ominous anticipation of Dick's own descent? – but Dick is intent on Rosemary and manages to get rid of him. Dick's phone call shows just how far gone he is in jealousy and desire, but Rosemary, in contrast, goes on writing to her mother when she has put the phone down. Her letter shows that she has been intent on her career too, a further indication that she is in control. Dick and Nicole, afraid of boredom, afraid of doing nothing, go to a play. Ironically, they present a fine outside to the world.

one of Tad's more savage cartoons Pseudonym of cartoonist Thomas Difzan (1877–1929).

the humbler poisons of France i.e. wines and spirits.

'**And two – for tea.**' Popular song of the period – romantic, sentimental.

XXII (pp.108–13)

The sudden and the unexpected mark the opening of this chapter. Has Abe gone? Narrative expectation rises in temperature, for Abe is capable of anything. Nicole nearly gets caught up in the mystery of Abe's presence in Paris and the fact that he has been robbed. Nicole is selfish, fed up with Abe anyway, escaping as usual into shopping and spending. Dick's investigation, the half-heard, distorted telephone voices and statements, combine to make the situation with Abe a grotesque one. Nicole reminisces about their past, but Dick is obviously becoming critical of her. The trouble is that he doesn't know how much Nicole knows about his *real* feelings for Rosemary. Nicole on the previous night referred pointedly to Rosemary as 'a child'. In the restaurant they are aware always of Americans, here the 'gold-star muzzers' who have come over as a tribute to their dead in the war. The effect on Dick is to cause his hilarity to give way to American nostalgia. This shows how volatile he can be. Potently, the chapter ends on the note of his obsession with Rosemary in the reminder of her behaviour with the boy on the train – 'Do you mind if I pull down the curtain?'.

sergent de ville Policeman.
carte d'identité Identity card.
chasseur See note on page 59.
muzzers Mothers, but in fact wives and relations mourning their husbands, sons, etc killed in the First World War.

XXIII (pp.114–16)

Abe is the worse for wear in the Ritz bar, still pushing his off-beat humour. He is playing games, as ever, in his alcohol-haze condition, making no move to go to the jail and have the man, whom he has wrongly accused of theft, released. With the news that Jules Peterson wishes to see him, Abe panics somewhat, gets up, and leaves. The tension builds up in the reader's mind as something is about to happen.

concessionnaire Licence-holder.
the France Luxury passenger liner.
Briglith Nonsense word.

XXIV (pp.116–21)

Meanwhile we return to Dick – this is Fitzgerald's cunning way of keeping the reader on tenterhooks. Dick makes for Rosemary, frightened within but possessed too. He is unable to resist her. When she opens the door to him we are aware that their minds are far apart. Rosemary's effect is seen in the image which conveys it – 'her body calculated to a millimeter to suggest a bud yet guarantee a flower'. After they have kissed she tells him they are both actors. She is right again, but the dramatic interruption of the knock at the door finds Dick covering up with fake conversation. The intrusion of Abe and Jules Peterson is followed by Abe's story – a compound of comedy, chaos and inefficiency. It is to have tragic repercussions. Before this there is an element of farce. The retrospect on Peterson strikes one as a rather clumsy narrative device in order to bring about the climax of the scene to come. Abe, who is offensive, continues alcoholicly jocular until his exit.

Miss Television i.e. outstanding picture (of beauty and prettiness).
Grant See note on page 65. Note that the phrase here is a typical
  piece of Abe's nonsense.

XXV (pp.122–6)

Rosemary continues to act, her exit being a study in professionalism. Once more Fitzgerald produces the unexpected. The discovery of the dead Jules Peterson initiates a sequence which has all the speed of a film, partly ironic it seems, since this incident could ruin Rosemary's career. Dick shows great presence of mind, and his efficiently furtive actions show how concerned he is on Rosemary's account. Here Fitzgerald combines contemporary fact – the reference to the Arbuckle case – with brilliant imaginative associations. For example, the hotel owner is whimsically called McBeth, a name associated with the most heinous of murderers. Deception comes easy to those who practise it. Dick, McBeth, the gendarmes, extend the chain of corruption and bribery. Worse is to come, for the insanity of Nicole has shown itself. She has given way to that other, darker side of her nature, just as she did at the party where she was seen by Violet McKisco. Tragedy is connected with tragedy, and Rosemary's part in this story closes with her trembling with relief. Collis Clay will arrive shortly so that she won't have to go to her room alone.

the Arbuckle case Fatty Arbuckle was a famous silent screen star
  whose career was virtually wrecked by a sex scandal.

Book I: Revision questions

1 What impression have you formed of Rosemary? Refer closely to the individual sections in your answer.

2 Trace Dick's falling in love with Rosemary. Why do you think this happens?

3 Write about any scene in the novel which you find interesting either because of its atmosphere or because of the way Fitzgerald presents it.

4 Compare and contrast McKisco and Abe North.

5 'We feel that Fitzgerald is the master of producing the sudden or the unexpected'. How far would you agree with this, judging from your reading of Book I?

6 Write about any aspect of the book which interested you, saying why.

Book II

I (pp.129–32)

Retrospect on Dick, going back to 1917, in order to integrate him psychologically in the reader's mind. He is a man of great ability, too valuable to be sent to the front. Even here though the war influence is vividly felt ('dying trunks'), and the author's irony is employed at the expense of his own country which 'bungled its way into the war'. We are taken even further back to 1914 and then forward again to live through Dick's deprivations as a student. All this contrasts tellingly with the later luxury he is to acquire. Here we see him in a different kind of dedication. The armadillo example almost prepares the way for Dick later abandoning what he does.

too much of a capital investment i.e. his abilities as a doctor would do better service for his country than if he were sent to fight.
Gorizia . . . the Somme . . . Aisne The fronts where the fighting was taking place in the Great War.
Oxford Rhodes Scholar A few scholarships for non-native English students were established at Oxford – Dick was obviously outstanding enough to get one of them.

the great Freud Sigmund Freud (1856–1939), the founder of
  psychoanalysis.
brief Summarize, abstract.
Fairy Blackstick In Thackeray's *The Rose and the Ring*. Thackeray
  (1811–63), the author of *Vanity Fair*, wrote this story for children.
Jung Carl Jung (1875–1961), great Swiss psychologist.
like Grant ... See note on page 65.

II (pp.132–40)

There are signs too (where Dick thinks of himself as a toymaker)
that he always has doubts about his chosen profession. He tells
Franz about his seeing Nicole, and we get the impression that
Dick is vulnerable and susceptible, not just to her beauty but to
her state of mind. The atmosphere of the clinic is well conveyed.
More retrospect embraces Nicole's letters to Dick. The first ones
show how disturbed she is (there is tension because we don't yet
know why), but a close look at them reveals her schizoid tendencies. Nicole's moods in her madness are traced through to what
appears to be a return to sanity. Again the section ends on a note
of tension, since Franz is obviously about to reveal what caused
Nicole's illness.

Cagliostro (1743–95), a charlatan implicated in swindles.
Kraepelin (1856–1926), German psychiatrist who practised in Munich.
basso Bass voice.
Armistice Signed 11 November 1918.
Je m'en fiche I don't care.
'plus petite et moins entendue' Very small and rare.
a twin six Schizophrenic.
alienist Psychiatrist.

III (pp.140–45)

The parallel between Warren and Dick is interesting: both are
attractive men. Warren fabricates his story and then breaks down,
the whole sequence tense with the relevation to come. Again we
are aware of the 'Daddy's Girl' motif, here with a terrible irony,
and we suspect the lies and the acting before the revelation. We
are also aware of another duplication, and that is that money does
not provide deep or lasting happiness. Dohmler handles things
well. We are left with the feeling that Nicole will not recover fully
unless Dick plays a positive part in her life.

'un homme trés chic' i.e. very handsome, impressive man.
run the submarine blockade This was undertaken by the Germans
during the First World War to stop American supplies reaching
Europe.

IV (pp.145–9)

This opens with the facts of the dramatic deal that has been
done – Warren is to keep away from his daughter for five years.
From now on Nicole becomes a case study, with Dick susceptible
both to the letters and the prospect of seeing her. In view of
Nicole's suspicion of men, it must be allowed that Dick has
already made a breakthrough. The two key emphases are Dick's
attractiveness to women as well as his determination to be a great
psychologist. There are a number of things against him but,
most markedly, himself.

Pestalozzi (1746–1827), Swiss founder of reformist elementary
education.
Alfred Escher (1819–82), Swiss statesman.
Zwingli (1484–1531), Swiss Protestant religious reformer.

V (pp.149–52)

There is some pathos in the fact that Nicole's first meeting here
with Dick is chaperoned. Nicole and the music combine to
awaken Dick emotionally and her mention of the popular songs
of the period plus her attitude seem to generate excitement. At
their next meeting Fitzgerald uses popular song to indicate their
romance. Nicole is making the most of herself and her influence.

Lothario Name of a character in a play by Nicholas Rowe, synonymous
with loose living, a deceiver or libertine.
They were so sorry, dear . . . Quotations from popular songs.
'A woman never knows . . .' From a popular song. Note its significance
to the plot of the novel.

VI (pp.152–6)

Dick is aware of the divisions within himself, though he is
obviously beginning to feel a little possessive about Nicole. She is
rich and worships him. At the same time he has big ideas about
his work. He is aware too, as Franz is, about what is happening

between himself and Nicole. Time is given a considered stress –
Dick looks back to his childhood and forward to Dohmler's
death – and he recognizes in Dohmler a superior individual.
Note Dohmler's directness over Nicole and her infatuation with
Dick; he comes straight in. Dohmler and Franz in fact warn Dick
against the marriage he is already contemplating.

'Du lieber Gott! ...' 'For the love of God, please bring Dick a glass of
beer now.'

VII (pp.157–61)

The decision that Dick must 'eliminate' himself from Nicole's
presence means that the next meeting he has with her is full of
pathos. There are insights into Dick's control, but the overriding
emphasis is on Nicole's dependence on him and his awareness of
this. He tries to act either as a wet blanket, or as an encouraging
prop in her future, though telling her to be happy and to fall in
love smacks of insensitivity. But this outwardness conceals his
inward pain and his knowledge of her pain. She does not meet
him later and Dick concludes that she has got the message –
Franz reports her having been abstracted but not too much so.
The reader, like Dick, is left with a sense of anti-climax.

'Bonjour, Docteur ...' 'Good-day, Doctor. Good-day Sir. The weather
is fine. Yes, wonderful ...' The conversation in simple French belies
the suffering of the man who has been operated on. The simple
phrases are all he can manage.

VIII (pp.161–6)

Dick now becomes even more obsessed with Nicole, realizing
that his emotions are involved. He throws himself into a number
of activities, including his work, though this does not appear to
be practical; rather it is an attempt to impress himself. Dick's
bicycle tour leads to poetic description by Fitzgerald, but the
suddenness with which Nicole re-enters his life is effective. This
is so because the 'taint' of the clinic is gone. Dick is sensitive on
Nicole's account, fearing that he will be a reminder of the past.
At the same time, there is a superb sense of freshness – Fitzgerald's word – both of scene and of experience. After his

meeting with Nicole's sister, we note Dick's own helpless love for Nicole and her tortured love for him.

Irene Castle's With her husband Vernon, formed the most popular dance team before World War I (he was killed in 1918).

IX (pp.166–74)

Dick becomes the focus of attention, and Baby Warren thrusts herself upon him – she is predatory in her insistence. She is obviously interrogating Dick, and we suspect her motives; she is also something of a caricature herself. The irony is ever-present – for example, in Baby Warren's account of what she thinks happened to Nicole, and also in the orchestra playing 'Poor Butterfly', a song that epitomizes Nicole. There is a kind of grim comedy in the idea of 'buying' a doctor for Nicole, and notice that this is important in the structure of the novel, since Dick is going to allow himself to be bought. When he sees Nicole alone Dick still resists, despite her directness. But he cannot keep it up, and Nicole is in the ascendant. The storm is the climax of their love. But Dick is still annoyed by Baby Warren's note, which throws him and Nicole together deliberately. He does not know that she is innocent of intention, that she has found him too intellectual – this is another facet of the insistent irony.

Vanity Fair Famous society magazine.
Byron (1788–1824). Romantic poet noted also for his love affairs.
toothsome Pleasant, attractive.

X (pp.174–9)

Dick's conversation with Baby Warren shows that she is suspicious of him, Nicole's money being an obvious lure, but there is also some emphasis on their difference in class and status. There are ominous references to madness which is after all one of the themes of the novel. There is a suddenly effective switch into Nicole's consciousness which reflects the movements of her mind and emotion over a number of sequences – an economical way of marking the passage of time and registering its effects on the individual. It charts her relationship with Dick, but the fragmented monologues show too the dislocated nature of her mind in her reactions to situations – legal, loving, her pregnancy, their honeymoon on a boat, her fears and degrees of mental unbalance. The birth of Topsy (note the significance of the name; she was a slave in *Uncle Tom's Cabin*) is important because of the tensions it generates in Nicole. Nicole wishes to compete with Dick – or help him – by mastering a subject. There is an element of pathos about this. The ramblings and dislocations of Nicole's consciousness suggest that her illness runs like a subterranean current through her marriage to Dick.

Marshall Field (1834–1906) founded a famous department store in Chicago.
'Je m'en fiche de tout.' See note on page 74.
cameriere Chambermaid.
Pallas Athene In Greek mythology, the goddess of industry and war.
Mistinguett Legendary French cabaret artiste of the period.

XI (pp.179–86)

This marks a sudden switch in narrative time back to the present of Book I. Dick sees clearly into what is called the 'amorality' of Mrs Speers, realizing that only Rosemary counts in her mother's mind, his own feelings or Nicole's in any affair with Rosemary being irrelevant. Dick has moments of lucid self-honesty, as for instance when he tells Mrs Speers, 'My politeness is a trick of the heart'. He also tells Mrs Speers that he is in love with Rosemary. His knowledge that he only has a few ideas is good too – it almost prepares us for the fact that he really has nothing more to say about his medical research. His care of Nicole and the departure of Rosemary to continue as 'Daddy's Girl' are indicated. The flashback indicates Nicole's awareness of Dick's passion for Rosemary, and Dick's own anguish (the refrain lines again) at the thought of Rosemary and 'men'. There is a deliberate stress on the increasing frequency of Nicole's breakdowns. Dick has learned to treat her consistently despite the 'new coldness in his heart'.

a service stripe i.e. a promotion to indicate efficiency.
belladonna . . . mandragora Addictive drugs.
wagon-lit Sleeping car.
ceinture Inner circle (of the railway).
pousse Growth, development.

XII (pp.186–8)

Dick sees Nicole, but keeps her at a distance by describing his meeting with an eccentric acquaintance they both know. He wants to be alone and, when he is, plays a song on the piano which he associates with Rosemary. Sensitively he realizes that Nicole will guess why he is playing it. His deeper problems are financial: despite all his assertions of a little independence, Nicole has succeeded in buying him and owning him – this dependence is breaking his will to work anyway. The chapter closes with Nicole's current schizophrenic crisis overcome, and they go to the Alps.

Sigmund Freud See note on page 74.
Ward McAllister (1827–95), married a millionaire's daughter and became a leading light in New York society.

XIII (pp.189–97)

Baby has joined them on holiday, and the description focuses on her taste for death, her belief in the tragic destiny of her sister. Money is on the surface of the conversation, but Nicole's invitation to Dick to dance with 'ickle durls' seems to smack of her knowledge of his love for Rosemary. The irony of the author next plays over Baby Warren's reception of Franz, whom she treats with her 'second manner'. Dick is aware of a particular girl, but Franz's need to engage him in conversation is insistent. Dick's response to the offer of partnership – the chance to do his worthwhile work – is being overheard (and evaluated) by Baby. Dick brings her into the conversation – the need for money is paramount – but he is made very angry within by her cool insolence and her assumption of her power in whatever decision is made. It also shows Dick's increasing awareness of the price he is paying for having been bought. Despite his criticism of Baby he is on the point of succumbing to Franz's suggestion, even thinking that it will be good for Nicole.

Sturmtruppen Shock troops (ironic).
telemark A swing turn in skiing.
rich as Croesus The sixth century BC King of Lydia, the possessor of legendary wealth.
Jung ... Adler All psychologists.

XIV (pp.198–205)

The background of the war becomes temporarily the foreground in Dick's nightmare. Again the time clock is reset, and we find ourselves eighteen months on in Dick's clinical work. He is now thirty-eight, and he and Nicole are growing slowly apart, though ironically their home has gained some celebrity as a centre visited by every psychologist passing through the area. The switch to individual cases shows the demands being made on Dick. The interview with the woman whose disease and suffering have been inadequately diagnosed as 'nervous eczema' is harrowing in the extreme; we feel that, in acting as he has to – and Dick is an actor – Dick knows the inadequacy of what he is doing. There is a loss of faith.

a thing of beauty Another echo of Keats – 'A thing of beauty is a joy for ever.' (*Endymion*).
the Chopin Frederic Chopin (1810–49), great Polish pianist and composer.
gone i.e. out of her mind.
the whoopee cures Presumably unreliable ones.
Iron Maiden Form of torture where victim is confined in iron 'case containing spikes'.
a Pyrrhic victory One achieved at too great a cost (from Pyrrhus, who defeated the Romans but lost the pick of his army in doing so).
paresis Part paralysis, weakening of muscles.

XV (pp.205–12)

The pressures of Dick's job are brought out by the letter which accuses him of seducing the young girl. The accusation has got through to Nicole and precipitates a crisis. Her silence and set face are ominous. The fair therefore is not a relaxation; the atmosphere is charged with uncertainty when Nicole begins to run. Dick has to think for the children too, has to get them out of the way. Nicole, viewed sitting alone in the top boat of the ferris wheel, is a manifestation of insanity – she is hysterical. All the time of course there is the fear of suicide. She reveals her obsession – that Dick is interested in younger girls – but there is sublime pathos when, after her abuse, she appeals quietly to Dick for help. The car crash shows just how intense is the grip of madness and the attendant death wish in Nicole. All this prepares us for a corresponding break up in Dick – such responsibility is too much for anyone. He is also concerned about her need for alcohol – ironic in view of his own developing addiction.

a sudden awful smile The accompaniment to Nicole's change of mood – the symptom of her illness.
guignol See note on page 70.
'Est-ce que . . . gentille dame.' 'May I leave these children with you for two minutes? It's very urgent – I will give you ten francs.'/'But yes.'/ 'Now – stay with this nice lady.'
'La septième fille d'une septième fille . . . The seventh daughter of a seventh daughter was supposed to have psychic powers.
'Regarde moi . . . Anglaise!' 'Look at that – look at that English lady!'
Svengali The German–Polish musician who possesses hypnotic powers in George Du Maurier's novel *Trilby*.

XVI (pp.212–14)

The pressures having got to him, Dick really wants to go away on leave – of 'abstinence' as Franz calls it, and it is a reasonable Freudian slip of the tongue. He affects to be interested in a conference, and thinks ironically to himself about it. Exhilarated at the view from the aeroplane, he allows his imagination to wander. The whole flight is pathetic evidence of his need to be free. The demands made on him are consuming him.

Zwingli's miracles See note on page 75.
Rotarian A member of the Rotary club, originally a foundation of local businessmen.
Five-and-Ten Cheap store.

XVII (pp.215–19)

The meeting with Tommy Barban provides an escape within a society. Dick's sensitivity is such that he feels Tommy is critical of his 'waning vitality' – this is to become an obsession with him, as we shall see in the diving board incident later. The escape reflects the climate of the time, the division between East and West which has been accentuated in our own. This is followed by a typical Fitzgerald device: the suddenness of an announcement which carries its own drama – the death of Abe North. The dialogue is absolutely convincing as Dick registers his shock, and it is ironically followed by the discussion of trivialities – the club Abe crawled to, and being measured for suits.

Pilsudski (1867–1935), Polish statesman and leader (Prime Minister 1930–35).
speakeasy Shop selling illegal alcohol.

XVIII (pp.219–23)

Arrived in Innsbruck, Dick thinks of Nicole as being far away – he also thinks of her 'best self'. He is aware that he has lost himself, that he is both unacquisitive and yet has needs which are partly inherited – and also, worst of all, that he has sold himself. His vulnerability is shown here in his response to women: he turns away from the demands and responsibilities of Nicole; he turns towards and then away from the girl in the shadows and there is a teasing element of the might-have-been about the encounter. He climbs, divided against himself: it is almost as if Nicole's schizophrenia is contagious. Again comes the suddenness and shock, here the death of his father. A telling retrospect establishes his sympathetic affinity with that father and the humanitarian decencies of his past.

XIX (pp.223–8)

This opens with Dick's moving return home for his father's funeral. On the way back there is another surprise, a meeting with McKisco, now famous (but aware of his limitations) as a novelist. There is some delightful irony about Violet and her interaction with her husband. There is again the introduction of the unexpected when Dick gets off at Naples and shortly afterwards encounters Rosemary. He ponders on the past, then on the fact that now the age difference between them means that she will see him 'with discerning clarity'. As if to underline the contrast between past and present, Dick bumps into Collis Clay.

Goethe's (1749–1832), the great German poet, writer, statesman of Weimar.
couturières Dressmakers.
'The Grandeur that was Rome' Typical of the epics of the period. The quotation is from the American, Edgar Allan Poe (1809–49).
Corriere della Sera . . . città Americana. The Italian paper contains mention of a novel by Sinclair Lewis called *Main Street* in which the author analyses the social life of a small American city.
tied up in bags i.e. doing what (she) wants them to do.

XX (pp.228–33)

The phone interruptions to Dick's meeting with Rosemary create another tense atmosphere, almost as if they are never going to be at peace. When 'she lowered the lights for love' we are reminded of that refrain line – the blind being pulled down on the train – which haunted Dick for so long. Three years have passed, and their coming together, without consummation, registers the changes in both of them. We are reminded that Dick now has particular needs of reassurance, and we see that she is acting up for him. The set and the reactions of those on it form a grotesque background to Dick and Rosemary, and it is obvious that the actor Nicotera is interested in Rosemary.

Valentinos Rudolph Valentino, a famous actor of the silent screen,
noted for his romantic roles.

XXI (pp.233–9)

The meeting with Baby Warren is unexpected, but her reactions to Nicole's situation are predictable. As usual she tries to influence Dick, trying to get him (and Nicole) to settle in London. She employs the usual reflex bait of the Warren family's money. He is moved to laughter by her unconscious debasing of human relationships when she says that it could easily be arranged for Nicole to marry somebody else, though such is her egoism that she is smoothly switched to the coy contemplation of her own affairs. Despite his irony at her expense, Dick finds something to admire in Baby. After that he tortures himself over Rosemary's past affairs, and also shows how jealous he is of Nicotera. Rosemary's tearful reaction shows him that he has failed his own image – 'I don't seem to bring people happiness any more.'

Michael Arlen (1895–1956), novelist of Armenian origin, wrote novels
of English society life in the 1920s.
snow over i.e. obscure, cover.

XXII (pp.239–46)

Dick's mood here is calculated to provoke trouble – he is looking for it. He spars verbally with Collis Clay in his condemnation of the place and then, when the note arrives from Rosemary, rejects its implicit invitation by saying that he cannot be found. Dick's determined prejudices are made worse by the ride in the taxi. His drinking leads to confrontation and, as ever, he has an eye for the pretty girl, but his mood is not helped by Clay criticizing the fact that he (Dick) does not practise as a doctor. There follows one of the most violent incidents in the book, the row over the taxi fare first and then the viciousness, the suddenness of the assault.

We have seen Dick's steady decline for some time now, but this chapter underlines Dick's fall.

frail Prostitute.
where Keats had died Another reminder of Fitzgerald's attachment to the romantic poet, who died in Rome at the age of 25 and was buried there with the simple inscription 'Here lies one whose name was writ in water.'
a quick trick i.e. an easy conquest – sexual invitation.
'Quanto a Hotel . . .' 'How much to the Quirinal Hotel?' '100 lire. . .' 'Thirty-five lire at most.'
'Alors. Écoute . . . va au Quirinal.' (paraphrase) 'Right. Listen. Go to the Quirinal Hotel. It's somewhere to sleep. Listen. You're on your own. Pay what the driver asks. Do you understand?' . . . 'Ha, I won't' . . . 'What?' . . . 'I'll pay 40 lire. That's enough . . .' 'You have assaulted the driver, like this. You're lucky to be free. Pay what he asks – 100 lire. Go to the Quirinal.'

XXIII (pp.247–56)

The summoning of Baby Warren to the aid of Dick is not without its comic elements, and strangely she has been thinking of him before she gets the news of his arrest. Baby reveals her determination (that we suspected) and also her authority, though she has to face obstinacy, apathy and apprehension. The whole chapter is full of speed and activity, the prose and the dialogue reflecting both. There is a bubbling comedy in the description of the diplomatic official, his bagged moustache the major part of his grotesquerie which is emphasized by the pink cold cream. His speech is the kind of bureaucratic palliative which is calculated to incite someone of Baby's temperament. This grotesque is succeeded by the reclining nude of Collis Clay (Baby is too hurried really to notice). Baby pulls status and wealth on the apathetic consul. As ever, she wins. Dick, though down, has sufficient spirit to poke fun at Swanson, and almost succeeds in getting himself into trouble again. Even worse, he affects to be the rapist the crowd are waiting for – Dick is still taking on the world, rebelling against himself, perhaps from the deep shame of failure.

carabinieri Guards.
'Non capisco inglese' I don't understand English.
semper dritte, **dextra** and **sinestra** Keep straight ahead, right and left.

Book II: Revision questions

1 Do you think that the flashback sequences here – about Nicole and Dick – would have helped your understanding better if they had been placed at the *beginning* of the novel? Give reasons for your answer.

2 Write a detailed character study of Nicole, bringing out her problems and her actions clearly.

3 Judging from this book, how far is Dick responsible for his own decline and fall?

4 Write short character studies of Baby Warren and Mrs Speers.

5 Here and in Book I there are references to the War. How important are they to our appreciation of the novel and the behaviour of Dick?

6 Write an account of the coming together of Dick and Rosemary. How far does this contribute to Dick's decline?

7 There are some dramatic incidents in this sequence. Pick out any two and write about them critically, saying whether you consider them successful or not.

Book III

I (pp.259–62)

Kaethe's view of Nicole – that she is less ill than everyone thinks she is – prepares us for Nicole's ultimate recovery and movement into life. Kaethe realizes the divisions between herself and Nicole, and with Dick's return she realizes what is happening to him. She puts it superbly in a succinct phrase – 'Dick is no longer a serious man.' She is, however, very obviously jealous of Dick on her husband's account, respecting and loving him – Franz – for his dedication, which Dick is now conspicuously lacking.

Norma Talmadge The actress sister of Constance Talmadge. See note on page 59.

II (pp.262–72)

This sequence is full of action and revelation – notice how successfully Fitzgerald keeps the narrative pot boiling. Dick lies to Nicole about what actually happened in Rome. He gets caught up in the death of the woman artist, takes on the father-son problem (this is a structural duplication of the relationship between Nicole and her father), but he is curiously detached, absorbed by his own life and his reflections. He thinks back to the period of 'the broken universe of the war's ending'. Consequently Royal Dumphrey's introduction reawakens that past, though Royal's role is obviously functional, for he brings news of the serious illness of Mr Warren. Dick has to try and cope with the Spaniard and with the confession of Mr Warren. Kaethe's reaction when she gets the news nearly precipitates another crisis with Nicole. The drama continues with Warren's sudden departure, the arrival of Nicole, and Dick's seeing ominous signs in her expression.

bordello Brothel.
'The Wedding of the Painted Doll' Music again used here with ironic associations.

III (pp.272–6)

Dick's downward career continues with the removal of the Australian patient by his incensed and bigoted parents. As a result of this self-examination, Dick becomes his own patient. When he confides in Franz, the latter invokes the past by referring once again to a leave of 'abstinence'. He is acute enough to see what is happening to Dick. He demonstrates it quickly by at once accepting Dick's offer to pull out, a sure indication that he knows that his partner's heart is not in the job.

IV (pp.277–85)

With the supposed freedom he has bought by leaving, Dick becomes more interested in his children. He takes a particularly strong line with regard to Topsy, refusing to bring her up as 'Daddy's Girl' (and doubtless mindful of Nicole's situation with her father). There is a satirical and ironic account of how, because of the increase in money, the Divers travel in state, and live up to their (supposed) status. The princeliness is accentuated by Mary North's new rank, acquired by her marriage. Dick is cynical about her self-evident ambition – 'If Europe ever goes Bolshevik she'll turn up as the bride of Stalin.' Dick continues to drink, there is money talk, while the Lanier bathwater incident provokes a crisis which shows Dick on a short fuse and exposes the superficiality of the civilized behaviour of the families to each other. It is another sign of the worsening relationship between Dick and Nicole too. At the same time, Dick shows (end of chapter) that his sense of humour is not in abeyance, yet 'you can divorce a child' carries the poignant irony of what is to happen to the family too.

Italian pilgrimages of Lord Byron The latter spent much time in Italy where he acquired, apart from the love of the language and history, a mistress in the form of Teresa Guiccioli.

Mason-Dixon The line between Maryland and Pennsylvania, the division before the Civil War between the free and slave states.

V (pp.285–96)

The next incident is the row with Augustine and her dismissal – Dick is again provocative and provoked. An element of farcical comedy runs through the whole exchange despite the seriousness of what it reveals about Dick. He is pondering behind his silence, Nicole realizes, and she is now daring to criticize him. Dick we feel is intent on proving himself and being accepted once more into society, hence the trip to the Golding yacht. It has far-reaching effects. Firstly, it brings Nicole into contact with Tommy Barban, and this leads to her later running away with him. We meet the socialite and perverted Lady Caroline, later to figure in a degrading incident with Mary (indicative of perversion). Dick is determinedly anti-British, the background music is a childish indulgence, and Dick is aware of social condemnation (via Lady Caroline). There is a scene between Nicole and Dick which hints that he is thinking of making the break. We note Nicole's loyalty when Tommy suggests that Dick is drinking too much.

bastide Small house.

Salaud! Dirty dog, skunk.

'Mais pour nos héros . . . les grandes compositions.' But for heroes like us we need time. We can't indulge in petty heroics – we need greater situations.

Ronald Colman Famous English romantic actor who went to Hollywood to star in American films.

Corps d'Afrique du Nord North African Corps.

a mille Swiss A thousand Swiss francs.

a Danny Deever monotone An association picked up from the Kipling poem with its refrain line, 'For they're hanging Danny Deever in the morning.'

'Quelle enfanterie . . . Racine!' 'What childishness . . . He sounds as if he's reciting Racine' (French classical playwright).

VI (pp.296–300)

The morning after finds the divisions between the three of them – for Tommy is there – clearly spelled out. Nicole is made happier by the knowledge of Tommy's love for her, it is almost as if she is finding herself for the first time. Brooding on her interest in Tommy, she overhears a conversation about seduction which undoubtedly points her mind and emotions in the sexual direction she wants them to go. The result is that Dick notes her concern for Tommy. The chapter ends on a note of expectation with the news of Rosemary's arrival – it is almost as if fate is moving Dick and Nicole apart.

VII (pp.300–12)

Nicole senses that Dick is now desperate – notice how completely we have been brought over to see things from Nicole's angle. She is bewildered because she does not understand his motivation, what lies behind his growing indifference. She is astute enough to work out that being with his children affords Dick a kind of protection. There is a terrible irony in the beach trip being for him 'like a deposed ruler secretly visiting an old court'. She is aware too of the past and of Dick's search for Rosemary, and watches the 'old game of flattery' springing up between them. Nicole sees into and through his endeavour to impress Rosemary – his failure is symbolic of his failure in life and, in different ways, with Rosemary and Nicole. The latter's annoyance reflects her growing away from Dick. The meeting with Mary is something of a humiliation for Dick. After more tension in front of Rosemary, more drinking from Dick, they come together in the evening feeling 'empty-hearted towards each other'. Nicole has earlier felt herself cured, and with Tommy Barban's call after Dick leaves she feels the warmth in herself.

an Anita Loos heroine Loos was the author of a best seller of the period which was subsequently filmed – *Gentlemen Prefer Blondes*.

Faits Accomplis i.e. Mary turned up when things were already over/decided.

'Thank y' father-r . . .' Another song with poignant associations in view of the imminent splitting up of Dick and Nicole.

VIII (pp.312–20)

Nicole's determination to have an 'affair' is stressed as she prepares herself for Tommy: we feel that in her mind it will represent maturity, recovery, completeness. Initially she is aware that she feels the ghost of Dick, a natural feeling since she has been dependent upon him for so long. Their coming together is different from anything she has known or expected, and is complemented by the strident goodbyes of the sailors' girls, a coarse equivalent to their own consummation in the hotel room. By the end of the chapter, as Nicole and Tommy leave to go back to her children, she realizes that she has broken from the dependence on Dick. There is no interpretation or qualification of what she has done.

a fighting Puck The sprite or goblin thought to haunt the English countryside – mischievous character in Shakespeare's *A Midsummer Night's Dream*.

poules i.e. birds (girls)

Kwee Can we?

IX (pp.321–4)

Dick's return flusters Nicole, but he tells her that Rosemary didn't grow up (was she always 'Daddy's Girl' in his mind?). Nicole lies to herself about the past, then realizes that she has betrayed Dick by doing so. When she approaches him she soon learns that he is no longer concerned with her – as he eloquently puts it, he is trying to save himself. In a brilliant piece of analysis Fitzgerald exposes Nicole's consciousness as she wins the battle with herself: she has to let go, does so in great personal anguish, and Doctor Diver is freed, as she is freed, from the trap of her condition, their marriage, his responsibility.

X (pp.324–9)

The Mary North–Caroline Sibly-Biers incident is Dick's last rescue. Aptly he is compared to a priest in the confessional, but he brings all his humorous bluff to extracting them from the situation. In a sense the scene is a duplication of his own scene with the taxi drivers and the police, with Dick playing the Baby Warren role. The sordidness of the situation, the irresponsibility and self-indulgent emphasis, is not lost on the reader. Ironically, it is the kind of joke which Dick himself would have initiated and appreciated in the past.

'mais à qui est-ce que je parle?' 'But to whom am I speaking?'
Lord Henry Ford A deliberate distortion, just like John D. Rockefeller Mellon. By using the names of millionaires and the founder of the Ford motor company, Dick is blinding the man with social snobbery and wealth.

XI (pp.329–33)

The prison of the hairdresser's – another grotesque little sequence. The interruption by the seedy American, remembered in Paris five years earlier, plus the commotion of the cycle race, make the interchanges between the two men almost humorous. Tommy is on his high horse, but Dick, as Nicole recognizes, has anticipated everything since the day when she gave Tommy the camphor rub.

'Il n'y a plus . . .' 'We haven't any black and white. We only have Johnny Walker.' 'That'll do.'

'Cessez cela! allez ouste!' 'Stop that! Off you go!'
'Elle doit avoir . . .' 'She needs me more than she needs you.'
'L'amour de famille' 'Family love'

XII (pp.334–7)

There is a terrible pathos which runs throughout this chapter, and it begins with Dick spending all this time with his children. The real tragedy of the break-up is seen in his loss of family and the loss of self – the latter has already occurred. We can see that Nicole is still drawn towards him, almost as if she has assumed his role towards her and wants to protect him. Baby exercises her usual authoritarian practice. Even in conversation with Mary Dick plays up to the image of his old self. As he flirts with her though, he feels the laughter inside himself – he is still playing, projecting images. The final pathos is Nicole's wishing to go to him, and Tommy restraining her.

A.P. Associated Press.
an authenticated Hapsburg A genuine descendant of the family which ruled Austria and the Holy Roman Empire.

XIII (pp.337–8)

The final brief note, which indicates that he has disappeared completely from the society he once ruled. It is a continuing downward movement, yet we wonder if Nicole will ever forget what he has done for her. Their parting, their failure, is somehow the failure of the time, of the period, the post-war escape into superficial living-it-up as distinct from just living.

like Grant's in Galena See note on Grant, page 65.

Book III: Revision questions

1 Trace the various incidents in Dick's downward path. Do you find them convincing? What has happened to Dick?

2 What changes do you note in Nicole during this period? Does she want to leave Dick?

3 What aspects of this Book do you find most moving and why?

4 What do you think Fitzgerald is telling the reader in this sequence? What kind of comment is he making on society?

5 Write about any scene or situation in this Book which you find interesting.

Scott Fitzgerald's Art in *Tender is the Night*
The characters

Dick Diver

Organizer of private gaiety, curator of a richly encrusted happiness.

The name itself is significant, since Dick dives to the depths, ironically both of degradation and of knowledge, surfacing scarred by the experience on the one hand, and bringing back his discoveries on the other. Since he is the centre of the novel, any study of him could run to book length. In order to avoid that, the main outlines of his rise and fall are given here, and the committed reader will examine the novel for evidence to support these evaluations. Dick is an outstanding student, his abilities so recognized that he is not sent to the trenches in 1917. The recollection of war and what he has missed haunts him from time to time during the course of the action. He endures much privation in order to succeed in his studies, but even this does not make for maturity. He is the American in Europe, clean-living and romantic, but always, we feel, suspect when it comes to responsibility. This may seem a little paradoxical because of his ability to take responsibility for Nicole, but in a sense he is failing to take the responsibility of dedication to a career in medicine. It is also, in a curious way, unfair to Nicole, since the doctor-husband means that she is always a patient as well as a wife. This will be examined later in relation to Nicole.

Briefly, Dick is tempted by the genuineness of his own feelings to marry Nicole. He does this against advice (some of which comes from within), and he reaps the whirlwind. Determined to be financially independent of his rich wife, he finds it practically impossible. He sees himself and the situation ironically, but there is nothing he can do about it. He becomes the major charmer in a society set, enjoys the projection of his own image, seeks sensation instead of intellectual and practical achievement and becomes, in a word, a glamorous focus for those seeking sensation who know that he will provide it. The idealist has failed; the dreams the young Dick fed on have reached a terrible delusive expression. Dick is an entertainer who, because of his wife's money, can pick and choose his own audience.

The arrival of Rosemary finds him at the peak of this world. The fact that he is drawn towards her, despite all his good intentions not to be, shows how fragile that world is. What has become his natural condition – to be the focus of all eyes – is now accentuated by the desire to impress Rosemary. It must be said at once that he has the kind of personality that conveys warmth and interest, some of it spurious, but with the advent of Rosemary he too feels the constraints of the marital trap (and inwardly of course his own sense of failure – he is a bought man who is a kept man). He has poise, the ability to be interested in others and to flatter them by so being and, seen from Rosemary's angle, he is protective too – and desirable. Yet Dick's craving for sensation is often followed by an attendant depression. He knows what he is doing to himself, though only Nicole can be said to be aware of this. Dick loves the limelight, but it is inevitably followed by the darkness of self-knowledge. Dick has made his own world for the approval of others. Rosemary subscribes to that world by making an idol out of him. But Dick is soon aware of the trap and the fact that he is drawn to Rosemary. He fights it, but in a sense her youth never leaves his emotions and his inclinations. He is partly frustrated by being aware of his age in relation to her, and at the same time the divisions within him register because Nicole becomes even wealthier while he drifts farther from work. From now on we can see the beginnings of disintegration.

The clinic gives him an opportunity to rediscover himself and his dedication to medical science, though he is still conscious all the time of the trap with Nicole. Interaction with the patients, particularly the woman-artist whom he half loves, does not assist his balance – in fact they emphasize the divisions. Crisis point is reached when Dick is accused by the manic-depressive of seducing her daughter. Nicole half-believes this, and it precipitates her jealousy (the initiator of this was Rosemary) which leads to the breakdown in the fairground. Her pathetic 'Help me, help me, Dick' calls forth his anguish and underlines the extent of his sacrifice. Almost immediately afterwards there comes the terrible car incident when Nicole's 'mad hand' nearly kills all of them. Dick takes his 'leave of abstinence', meets Tommy Barban and is pushed on down by the news of Abe North's murder. He becomes increasingly aware of other women but is further disturbed into morbid retrospect and nostalgia by the death of his father. As if this is not enough, he re-meets Rosemary, and although his sense tells him that he is now much too old for her his feelings tell him something different. Eventually their affair is consummated, but afterwards it becomes apparent that she is having an affair anyway with her leading man. Dick is jealous and possessive, just as he was in the past.

Dick realizes that he has failed his image – he thinks of himself as the Black Death now that he doesn't give anyone happiness. He drinks heavily, argues with the cabmen, assaults the man at the police station, and has to be bailed out by Baby Warren. His feet are now on the floor of degradation. When he returns to the clinic he tells Nicole 'an expurgated version' of what happened in Rome; the next crisis is the death of the artist-woman, and Dick's turning off from the boy who was known at Cambridge as 'the Queen of Chile'. Events conspire to make themselves too much for him – there is the news of Mr Warren's imminent death, then the withdrawal of the Australian boy because of Dick's drinking. Franz knows that Dick's heart is no longer in the clinic: Dick is further demoralized by the ease with which he is able to withdraw from his responsibilities here. The bathwater sequence and Mary's contempt for him make things worse: only Dick's sense of humour saves him at such times. The row with Augustine, the row with Lady Caroline, his observation of the camphor rub, the showing off – and failure – before Rosemary, all these mark the final steps of the descent. There is the last pathos of nursing time with his children, the intense loneliness as he tries to find his identity, his late rescuing gesture involving Mary and Lady Caroline. His career is not biding its time. It is finished.

Nicole

Her lips drew apart into a sudden awful smile.

Nicole Diver, née Warren, is a mental patient. The focus of her attention is Dick in his capacity as a doctor. She is attracted to him – he is young, handsome, sympathetic – and writes to him while she is a patient in the clinic. We learn what has caused her mental illness, a form of schizophrenia, when her father breaks down and confesses his incest with her. She herself is very attractive, and we have to read Book II of the novel carefully in order to see exactly how Dick becomes fascinated by her. He always has an interest in younger girls anyway. Nicole's fear of men becomes transferred to the hero-worship of Dick. Her vulnerability, her fragility, calls forth a chivalric and protective response in Dick. She is also sexually attractive, but basically she arouses Dick's compassion and, against advice, he assumes the role of husband and nurse which constitutes their marriage. Nicole is rich, but she gives herself to Dick in worship. Her money comes to play a large part in their lives, for Nicole drains Dick emotionally through her relapses, like the one mentioned above at the fairground and in the car, or the earlier one in the bathroom which was witnessed by Violet McKisco. Ultimately, and convincingly too, she comes through to a kind of independence in which she chooses to go off with Tommy Barban. But we remember how she tries to keep in touch with Dick afterwards by getting news of him, and we remember too how her last sight of him on the terrace moves her to go to him though she is prevented from doing so by Tommy. Nicole knows in her heart what Dick has done for her, though she does not understand the enigma of his personality.

There is no doubt that she is jealous over Rosemary (though outwardly she is quiet, reserved, somewhat reticent) and that, pushed by circumstances, she is hysterical and unbalanced, witness her reaction to the letter she gets accusing Dick of seduction. She is capable of generous outgoing action and of sharp sarcasm – on one occasion when Rosemary comes back into their lives she snubs her. Her eyes sometimes give her away, as does her mouth; there is an unnamed fear in the eyes, and a tautness of expression in the mouth. Her wealth means that she indulges in spending sprees, almost by right. The strength of the sexual attraction she exerts upon Dick – complemented by his upon her – is seen in Book I, XII where their immediate needs are overheard by Rosemary. Nicole in Book I appears capable of enjoyment, but when the Riviera scene gives way to the clinic experience because of Dick's work, one feels that the associations – the recall of her own past as patient – are too much for her. She is trapped just as Dick is trapped, and this helps to precipitate her outbreak of violence.

The last sections of the novel mark another transference, here into the consciousness of Nicole as Dick goes into decline. Before that we have an inkling of her possible recovery – or has she already recovered in a sense? – when Kaethe observes to her husband that Nicole is using her illness in order to exert her will.

She grows into a new awareness of her sexual power when they meet Tommy Barban. The latter attracts her – it is an invitation to a new life. Her moral debate is a short one, for if other women can take lovers so can she. Yet still there is a feeling of guilt about Dick, and something of dependence, insecurity too. Nicole is a fascinating study, since Fitzgerald cunningly switches perspective. We are aware in Book I that there is something wrong with Nicole though we don't know precisely what. Book II gives us the integration and the explanation, the case history behind the superficial life we have just seen. And in Book III the focus is on Nicole as she comes out on the other side of madness into a kind of maturity. She is a complex character, but in presenting her through the sequence indicated above, Fitzgerald gives her a convincing completeness.

Rosemary

Wound yourself or him – whatever happens it can't spoil you because economically you're a boy, not a girl.

'Daddy's Girl' has made Rosemary, but her mother has, so to speak, had her in training from an early age. When we first see her she is nearly eighteen – young, vital, impressionable – looking for experience and forcefully embracing it. She is very much aware of her own image as a film star – aware rather than conceited – inquisitive too about the social groupings on the beach. She soon becomes involved and falls in love with Dick – but she is ready to fall in love anyway, almost as a reward for her hard work and achievement. She confides the suddenness of this to her mother, just as she tells her everything always. She becomes fascinated by both the Divers, is moved by Dick's courtesy, attention and concern. She begins to worship. But Rosemary, who is nothing if not dutiful, does what her mother requires of her career-wise, and goes to meet Earl Brady.

At the party she tells Dick she loves him – this is not guile, but direct impetuosity. Then, unable to sleep, she gets caught up in the duel. She has acquired the craving for sensation. When she and the Divers go to Paris, this craving is accentuated. Her overhearing Dick and Nicole expressing their sexual desire for each other excites her, but when she goes shopping with Nicole she marvels at the fact that she can keep Dick waiting – and even wishes that she could go to him herself. The visit to the war graves finds her moved at the contemplation of the great losses. Later Dick is 'chilled by the innocence of her kiss'. She throws herself at Dick – 'it was one of her greatest roles' – is abandoned, pleading, and frustrated. But she is also disciplined – the hairbrushing ritual has to be gone through if she is to maintain her economic potential. She shows later a streak of determination which matches the hardness of her nature – she reveals, without thinking, what she feels for Dick by saying that she has arranged a screen test for him. The meeting with the 'three cobra women' brings Dick and Rosemary closer together (she is upset by it). But with their kisses of separation just past, Rosemary, typically, writes to her mother from conscience, mainly because she has not missed her at all. Rosemary has had a kind of innocent experience earlier, as we know from Dick's jealous reaction to Collis Clay's story. Rosemary's later letter to her mother shows that she has an eye to the main Hollywood chance. It is just as her mother would wish. That main chance is nearly put at risk, and only Dick's presence of mind preserves it. The removal of the Peterson body ensures that Rosemary will live up to her contracted image of being 'Daddy's Girl'.

Rosemary at twenty-two meets Dick at thirty-eight. He is the ideal, we are told, that she has measured other men by. But the change is apparent too. Their consummation is anti-climactic, or so it appears, and she obviously goes with Nicotera too. Rosemary is romantic. Frustrated in the incompleteness of their relationship, she asks why they just couldn't live on the memory. Much later, with Dick in decline, she telegrams her arrival. Dick is moved to undertake his great showing off. He fails. Rosemary, five years after her infatuation, plays up to him, but when Mary comes over to talk it is Rosemary, the celebrity, who is the centre, not the fallen Divers. Dick's final words about her are that she hadn't grown up. But we are left with the strong impression that Rosemary has been coached throughout life for success, and that she cannot shed the need for that success by putting any personal relationship first. In any case, Dick has gone beyond her in his downward spiral towards obscurity.

Other characters

Fitzgerald has a great gift for characterization of an arresting and idiosyncratic nature. *Baby Warren* is just such a character, with her insensitivity and her assumption that money can buy not only anything but anyone (in a terrible way she is right). Ironically Dick is bought by Nicole's money, though Baby really disapproves of him because he lacks the status that she requires in her world. It would be true to say that she has no time for Dick's world, whether it is merely the medical one or the Riviera one. She lacks warmth and humanity, though she appreciates the fact that Dick takes Nicole off her hands. Dick sees her ironically throughout, and this means that we as readers respond to her through his reactions. He thinks of her as selfish: he is right. Although we may feel saddened by the fact that her English lover died in the war, we cannot help feeling that Baby (there is deliberate irony in the choice of name) is the cold, hard, determined American woman of means who knows that she can control men. She tries, we feel, to reduce them in the process. On one occasion she acts positively for good, and this is when she bails Dick out in Rome. Here her determination stands her in good stead, though we may smile at the incongruity of her militant behaviour. She is unscrupulous; even Dick has to grin at the easy way she is prepared to push him aside so that Nicole can marry again. The key word here is 'arranged', for she knows that with her money anything can be bought or changed. Morality never enters into it.

Mary North, later the Contessa di Minghetti, comes into unexpected prominence in the latter part of the novel. Her second marriage alters her status, and with it her relationship to the Divers, for she is now in an ascendant greater than theirs had been when she was worried about her hard-drinking husband. She can now stand on her own dignity and that of her new husband. Lanier's version of the bathwater incident provokes a row in which she puts down Dick and gets something of the sharp end of his tongue as a result. Although Dick finds her boring now, it is symptomatic of his own decline and of her rise that he should do so. When she re-meets the Divers on the beach we see how far 'little Mary North' has come, for she is able to snub them. In yet another ironic emphasis, her own fall is only averted by Dick's power and presence of mind. Mary and the probably perverted Lady Caroline pretend to be French sailors and pick up two girls, one of whom comes from a supposedly respectable background, so that there is the threat of trouble. Mary, unlike her companion, is frightened at her own behaviour (is she perverted or merely seeking sensation?) and doubtless about her husband's reaction should she be arrested. Dick saves her from this, and in their last conversation we realize that Dick is playing with her. She tells him that she, like everyone else, loved him, the implication being that if he'd wanted an affair with her while she was married to Abe he could have had it. But Dick is now living in his fallen present not his elevated past, and the Mary who is with him is almost unrecognizable as the Mary we hardly knew in that past to which she refers.

Mrs Speers, Rosemary's mother, has succeeded in pushing her daughter along the road to success. In many ways Rosemary is 'Mummy's Girl', always confiding in her mother, for example, telling her straightaway that she has fallen in love with Dick. But Mrs Speers, having done all she can for Rosemary (she is, after all, a star), seems to want her daughter to have the experiences of love which are necessary to maturity. Mrs Speers approves of the Divers, more specifically of Dick, and emphasizes Rosemary's economic independence of men. But we do feel that perhaps she goes over the top when she advises her daughter to 'wound yourself or him' (Dick), and it is this courting of emotional experience that leads her to advise Rosemary in the middle of the night to see the duel if she wants to. When Rosemary goes to Paris with the Divers, the first real break from her mother, she writes telling her all the news as it happens. But she also feels guilty on occasions when she realizes that she hasn't thought of Mrs Speers. Dick meets her later, and realizes that she is inviolable in her detachment from what is going on. He even seems to believe that she knows her own daughter well enough to be sure that she won't be hurt. Mrs Speers has earned her 'pension', and she doesn't appear to care about anything apart from her right to survive on it. She may, of course, have experienced life vicariously through her daughter's success, but she must take responsibility for Rosemary's lack of depth and real warmth. She is also responsible for Rosemary's calculating nature, which is derived from her own.

Other female characters are seen in passing, like *Violet McKisco* and her shock at what she saw of Nicole, which provokes the duel. Fitzgerald can bring a character very positively alive in a brief scene, as with *Augustine*, or the woman artist who is dying and for whom Dick feels so much. Even *Maria Wallis*, who says nothing but kills, is vividly evoked, while our passing acquaintance with the three cobra women is repugnant in its effect. *Lady Caroline Sibly-Biers* is directly revolting – loud, conceited, arrogant, unfeeling, used to her own way and determined to get it. She too has a craving for sensation and, probably, perversion. There is something predatory about her.

Of the male characters, two stand out – *Abe North* and *Tommy Barban*, though *McKisco* too has a positive identity. Abe stands out physically, he's a rotten swimmer, and Mrs McKisco says he is also a rotten musician, though he was potentially, we feel sure, a talented composer. He has a noble head, and he obviously reveres the Divers. He has, too, a good sense of humour – original and idiosyncratic. He enjoys baiting people somewhat, almost as if it is a game which underlines his ironic view of society. His remarks are little fireworks of wit, as when he tells the guests at the Diver party that he has got a moral code – by this he means that he is against the burning of witches. On the night (or morning) of the duel Rosemary notices that Abe is a little drunk (we later see his alcoholism much more clearly), but his joking continues as he acts as a second to McKisco. He is always kidding, like Dick sending up the Americans they see and even placing bets on the nature of repose. In Paris Rosemary notices the extent of Abe's alcoholism. There is a competitiveness between Abe and Dick (Dick is very fond of him), seen when Abe boasts pathetically, 'I'll have a new score on Broadway long before you've finished your scientific treatise.' Their careers are parallel in a sense – the drinking, the kidding, the failure with what is serious. In Paris Abe gives the impression of never having grown up. Mary is manifestly unable to cope with him. When he is about to leave he is in a sad state. He makes disagreeable remarks, his hands tremble so much that he can't light a cigarette. The most ominous thing about him is that he seems to have acquired the will to die. Mr 'Afghan' North does not leave Paris. He stays on, drinks heavily, creates the trouble which leads to the murder of Peterson. Much later, in terms of the structure of the novel, we learn that Abe has been killed in a speakeasy. There is a great sadness about his way of life, complemented by the manner of his death. It frees Mary into what on the face of it seems an unlikely second marriage.

Tommy Barban is tough, unscrupulous, in love with Nicole, strongly masculine. We are told that he is less civilized than the company he is in. He is sceptical, scoffs, but talks to Mrs Speers 'with an urbane fluency'. He quarrels with McKisco – before the quarrel that leads to the duel – saying quite simply that he is a soldier whose job it is to kill people. When Mrs McKisco refuses to stop talking about what she saw he presses for silence, and the determination to have a duel with McKisco emerges. Here his unscrupulousness shows, and when they both miss we feel that he is unhappy that honour has not been done. He declares himself unsatisfied. He bows coldly to McKisco after having talked to Abe. We are aware of his sexual potency and roughness when he re-meets Nicole. Their coming together is just at the right time for her, and in any case Tommy has ceased to like Dick. Dick meets him again in Munich where he is a 'ruler' and a 'hero'. We learn that he has been wounded and is vulnerable, but it doesn't show. He makes people afraid of him. He wears extraordinary suits and comments on Dick's 'waning vitality'. Later, on the Golding yacht, Nicole and Tommy are delighted at seeing each other. Tommy half boasts of his courage and his heroic qualities. He reveals that he holds some stock, and notices that Dick is now drinking. He seizes his opportunity, and when Nicole throws the camphor rub to him it is the sign of her preference. He is an immediate and fierce lover. He has got what he has craved for so long. He tries to provoke a scene with Dick but is outmanouevred, becomes pompous, and at the end restrains Nicole from going to Dick. We may not like him, but we have to recognize his vibrant determination. He sticks at what he aims to achieve, unlike Dick.

McKisco is on the edge of disagreement with his wife during his short but important presence in the action of the first section. There is talk about the plot of his novel and who is in it, but McKisco is defensive and Nicole reports the incident in which he rubs his wife's face in the sand. He thinks that Dick's appearance in the flesh-coloured lined drawers is 'a pansy's trick'. He gets rather drunk at the party and argues with Tommy Barban, thinking that he – McKisco – is superior to him because of his own intellectual quality. He 'spunkily' refuses to apologize to Tommy Barban, drinks himself into a state for the duel, arguing that he doesn't want to get too sober. He is 'reckless with brandy' by the time they fire at each other. He looks back on the incident with bravado, but is then violently sick. Unlike Dick and Abe he does not fall. The duel gives him a currency of self-respect, his novels are successful, he enjoys a vogue. His sense of inferiority has gone, though his wife's small-town ill-breeding hasn't.

Topsy hardly comes alive: there is something of Nicole in her reserve, but *Lanier* is well-drawn, speaking out, taking responsibility and inheriting his father's sense of humour. The homosexual *Royal Campion* is camp caricature, but *Gausse* comes alive in his own individual way. Passing characters have the brief stamp of truth, like the American in Paris with his convincing seediness, who is a symbol of Dick's own decline.

Themes

The themes of *Tender is the Night* are carefully integrated, one with another. The First World War (1914–18), with its unbearable loss of life, left its scar on the 1920s (the time-span of the novel, allowing for the flashbacks and the order, is roughly 1917–1930) and Fitzgerald captures the atmosphere of the time, particularly for those with money. There is the theme of failed idealism and achievement which concentrates on Dick, the brilliant young doctor who never completes his research, and is echoed in Abe North, whose musical compositions never see paper. Both lead lives of lost potential. These two major themes are intertwined throughout. Money and later alcohol lure Dick (alcohol destroys Abe), but there is also a sense in which these and other characters are lost in the post-war world. They seek sensation and spend money. They are Americans in Europe, living it up in an escapist and uncertain world. They are connected with violence, professional in the case of Tommy Barban, casual as a result of irresponsibility in the case of Dick. They can dazzle, as Dick does with Nicole, but the aftermath, like the aftermath of the war which is mentioned so many times during the text, is depression. Just as Nicole is ill, mentally ill because of her incestuous father, so the individual disease is translated into a society which becomes sick and meaningless. Just as in Keats' 'Ode to a Nightingale', which provides the title for the novel, there is a death-wish, so also this society has its own death wish, carrying within itself the seeds of its own destruction. Drinking, grotesque practical jokes and perversion are its areas of self-destruction: it is escapist, turning its back on the senseless butchery of the past and running the gamut of self-indulgence. There is an underlying moral tone in the novel as the activities of the Diver-led group are probed. And running parallel to that group is the world of the cinema, a new world of sentiment. The American soap factory which makes Rosemary a star and projects a romantic image of family life has, ironically, thrown up a breed of person who is threatening family values. (Baby indicates just how easy divorce is.)

There is a restlessness underlying all this which shows the

insecurity both of individuals and groups. Americans in Europe are bent on display, the parade of wealth, status, always seeking entertainment and making it happen for them. There is a strong emphasis on the sexual permissiveness of the age, though Dick and Nicole are apparently faithful to one another despite Dick's attraction to Rosemary. There is a degree of cynicism in the novel too, and the cases at the clinic, particularly that of the woman-artist, leave one with a feeling of despair. They are diseased within their prison, and outside is the larger prison of a society which is inflicting disease – moral and social – upon itself.

Settings

These are given a considered emphasis in the novel, and the committed student will examine each one to measure (a) its significance and (b) how it is linked to the themes indicated above and others which you may discover. For example, consider the movement in Book I. The Riviera scenes reflect the social groups, with the Divers at the top. It is an idle life in the sun, with parties which lead to arguments, violence and, in the case of Nicole, the revelation of her madness. The setting provides the ideal background in which to indulge one's cravings – it is the luxury against which you can make things happen. But what happens is not happiness – it is a simulation of living, a movement from responsibility. Next consider the Paris scenes (death, drinking, the twilit worlds of sensation-seeking groups), or a location like the visit to the war graves, or the set when Rosemary goes to see Earl Brady. Then have a look at the Swiss scenes, and focus particularly on the clinic and the atmosphere which is generated by it. Fitzgerald is the master of *scene*, whether it is setting only or whether it is more than that. You could look at the scene at the Gare Saint-Lazare as Abe waits to leave and Maria Wallis kills; or the scene in the hotel when Dick moves the body of Peterson to safeguard Rosemary's reputation (and contract); and the fairground scene when Nicole shows her frightening madness. All these are aspects of Fitzgerald's art, his clever linking of the actuality of place with the vividness of incident.

Style

Study the section commentaries and the notes carefully and you will pick up the salient features of Fitzgerald's narrative methods and vivid prose. Firstly, Fitzgerald's style is beautifully economical and richly metaphorical at the same time. Similes and metaphors – telling, succinct – abound in his jewelled prose. Rosemary sees Nicole as 'a viking Madonna', her face shining through 'the faint motes that snowed across the candlelight' (Book I, VII). From time to time the author uses his own voice, rather in the manner of a Victorian novelist, to make his own comments or analogies, often of a literary, artistic or moral nature, or combining any of these with the irony which runs throughout the novel. Fitzgerald views his characters ironically and presents them with critical perspective and clarity. Sometimes the irony embraces them as they speak, for Fitzgerald is the master of dialogue – his ear is tuned to ordinary exchange and the speech emphasis which carries its own nuance or innuendo. Above all, Fitzgerald's style is vivid with actuality. In the scenes mentioned above I stressed this quality. He can convey atmosphere, more accurately, a variety of atmospheres. Thus the beach scenes (note the irony of the 'bright tan prayer rug of a beach') are bright with light, air, the way of leisure; but the worship itself, and the superficiality of it, carries its own moral comment. The style is often neat and clipped with epigrammatic force. We are aware of Fitzgerald's sophistication and the self-ironic depreciation of sophistication at the same time. The laughter is often grim. In the course of the novel Fitzgerald uses many styles. Think of the superb way he captures the fragments and movements in Nicole's mind through her letters to 'Mon Capitaine'. Think of how Abe North's speech conveys the cynical, witty, already disintegrating man. Think too of the idiosyncratic language of Franz or of Kaethe, or of the adoration of Dick which Rosemary expresses in the 'first love' stage of her experience. You will have noted the exploration of the consciousness which is seen in Dick's reiterative recall of what he was told by Collis Clay – '*Do you mind if I pull down the curtain?*', or the use of song to underline situation, or as comment on the contemporary scene. And if Nicole's letters are part of her case-history, then consider also Rosemary's letter to her mother from Paris, with its capitalization, its italics and its exclamation marks all indicative of her enthusiasm, her childishness and her need for drama.

Fitzgerald makes constant and effective use of 'vogue' expressions, fashions, real-life characters and events, places etc. All these are part of his ironic control and running wit; it is a style packed with relevance and immediacy.

General questions plus questions on related topics for coursework/examinations on other books you may be studying

1 Give an account of the character of Dick Diver before he begins to go downhill.

Suggested notes for essay answer:
Introduction: background, upbringing, influence of father – student days – deprivation – brilliance.

Publications – recognized expertise – clinical experience – effect on him of Nicole – decision – strength of character in undertaking this – irony about money – wants independence – lets this become eroded.

Charm – practical joking – craving for sensation – restlessness – social centre – care of Nicole and children – greatly liked, admired, loved. Ironic attitude towards others – picks people up, drops them later – drawn occasionally towards others but loyal to Nicole until Rosemary – effect of Rosemary showing off.

Conclusion: points evident from the above plus great potential which is wasted in his cultivation of the social graces and a need for excitement, sensation, new experience.

2 For whom do you feel the most pity, Dick or Nicole? Give reasons for your answer.

3 Give an account of an important scene in Paris *or* on the Riviera *or* in Switzerland, bringing out its particular qualities and saying how it is typical of Fitzgerald's writing.

4 What do you find most interesting in the style of *Tender is the Night*? Quote from the book in support of what you say.

5 'The major theme of the novel is that of violence.' How far would you agree or disagree with this statement?

6 Characters reappear in the story – Mary, Tommy Barban, McKisco. Take two of these, and say what effects their reappearance has.

7 How important is the war to our understanding of *Tender is the Night*?

8 Read Keats's *Ode to a Nightingale*. What has it got in common with *Tender is the Night*?

9 Write an essay on Fitzgerald's use of irony in *Tender is the Night*.

10 'Dick is more seriously ill than Nicole.' Would you agree?

11 In what ways is *Tender is the Night* a moral book? Give your reasons.

12 Write a character study of Rosemary. How far does she change in the course of the novel?

13 'The overall effect is one of cynicism.' Would you agree with this assessment?

14 What do you find funny in *Tender is the Night* and why?

15 Write about anything in the novel which interests you and which is not covered by the questions above.

16 Discuss the treatment of madness in any book you have studied.

17 Write about a marriage which runs into difficulties in one of your chosen books.

18 Fitzgerald conveys the leisured atmosphere of a holiday in parts of this novel. Describe how an author creates a particular atmosphere in a book you know well.

19 Write about a character in one of your books who fails in life.

20 Which of the books you have read gives a full or vivid picture of life at a particular era, and how does the author achieve this?

Further reading

This Side of Paradise, F. Scott Fitzgerald (Penguin, 1963)

The Crack-Up and Other Stories, F. Scott Fitzgerald (Penguin, 1965)

New Essays on 'The Great Gatsby', Matthew Bruccoli (Cambridge University Press, 1986)

America, Alistair Cook (BBC Publications/Penguin, 1978)

F. Scott Fitzgerald: A Biography, André Le Vot (Penguin, 1985)